Shade

Susanna Grant

Photography Aloha Bonser-Shaw

gardening · nature · inspiration

Contents

03

Grow / p66
Discover just the
right plants for just
the right place

04

Care / p136
Learn to support
your plants and
help them thrive

Introduction

'If light is scarce then light is scarce; we will immerse ourselves in the darkness and there discover its own particular beauty'
Jun'ichirō Tanizaki *In Praise of Shadows*

This handbook is aimed at gardeners for whom sunlight is at a premium. It's a guide to encourage you to garden those small, oddly shaped or tricky areas that often get neglected because they don't receive much light. In it, I outline how shade works, why it's important for you and your garden and why it's necessary to green up more shady urban spaces. Choosing the right plants can be overwhelming and there are far more options available than I have included in this book, but the ones I have mentioned are my favourites, edited down over time to give a coherent aesthetic. I've tried to include plants that are fairly easy to source, as well as some more unusual cultivars. And I've also given advice that can be applied to a wide variety of situations and gardens, to give you the confidence to garden no matter what your space is like.

FOR THE LOVE OF SHADE

I blame Beth Chatto. It was her garden in Essex that really cemented my love of shade plants. I first visited with a friend one spring, around fifteen years ago, and we barely made it into the garden, spending most of the time wandering around the extensive nursery with two enormous trollies.

It was the first time I had seen so many plants for shade, let alone plants for different types of shade (rather than the usual small, samey selection of ferns, hostas and evergreens). There were so many options and varieties, and the flowers were delicate, bewitching: the nodding, creamy-white twin bells of Solomon's seal (*Polygonatum* × *hybridum*), the open-faced wood anemone (*A. nemorosa*) and the blue flowers and silver-frosted foliage of brunnera. Often subtle, these are plants that require notice; they don't shout out at you, but once you've seen them they charm you.

I started to dream of turning my dark, unloved side return into a bosky retreat. It was the woodland flowers that really did it for me; there is something about woodland planting and the movement of light across foliage that suggests ancient glades and fairy tales, and it quickly takes me back to childhood. Woodland plants can work surprisingly well in small, urban, overlooked gardens or forgotten spaces; they might get lost in a larger garden, but can be the stars of a courtyard or window box.

ABOUT LINDA

I started Linda — a shady plant shop and planting design consultancy — in a friend's back yard off Hackney Road in 2018. It was a small, gloomy space that received very little light and was full of junk. Once it was cleared and the walls painted a lovely smudgy pink, I planted a series of large black containers with lush ferns, deadnettles (*Lamium*), astrantias, tiarellas, Mexican fleabane (*Erigeron karvinskianus*) and Japanese anemones (*A.* × *hybrida*). These then brought the bees, butterflies and hoverflies to the garden, which hadn't been there before. The more life that arrived in that tiny yard, the more interested I became in encouraging other people to plant up tricky outside spaces, those that are given up on because they don't get much light. Include a wide variety of plants in your garden and it encourages a wide range of pollinators, and these in turn attract other wildlife, which means you are connecting your space with other spaces around you and allowing the pollinators and wildlife to travel more freely. Shade provides shelter and depth, which even the smallest garden needs, and shade-loving woodland plants are particularly helpful for early pollinators.

Around the same time as transforming that yard and starting Linda, I began volunteering at Arnold Circus, a tiered community garden surrounding a Victorian bandstand that was built on the rubble

Left A collection of pots on different levels
at Linda **Right** A few leggy pelargoniums
in Linda's lovely greenhouse

of a 19th-century East London slum. Dry soil, large London plane trees and surrounding buildings on all sides make it a challenging space to garden, but it's an excellent place to learn that plants don't always do what we expect them to. Despite the conditions, the garden has giant clumps of established agapanthus that flower throughout late summer in dry shade, there are fig trees that fan their leaves out over the road, and there are sun-loving hollyhocks towering as high as our heads. I've learnt that it's always worth trying a plant in shade, despite the recommendations on its label – just make sure you water it well, mulch around it, pay attention to it and keep your fingers crossed.

I open Linda most Sundays from around mid-April to the end of September. It's an unusual shop environment – it still looks like someone's courtyard garden, but almost all of the plants in it are for sale. Plants are placed in groups so that people can get an idea of what works together – three pots of different heights filled with ferns or grasses in the corner of a small balcony can transform a barren space into something inviting. I'm only a couple of minutes' walk from Columbia Road Flower Market and people drift in all day, never quite knowing what to expect, but nearly always commenting on the lushness of the planting and the variety of plants, and expressing genuine surprise that so much can happily grow with so little direct light.

At one time, the yard used to get a few hours of direct light in the very late afternoon as the sun crept around the corner of Hackney Road, but that was before a monolithic development replaced the bingo hall opposite and stole the last sliver of light. Nevertheless, the plants still thrive, even the sun-loving scented pelargoniums are happy, if a little leggy. Together with the garden next door, the planting around the bike rack opposite, the patch of London rocket growing wild on the street corner and the roof terrace I planted across the road, the yard is part of a patchwork of green pitstops for pollinators. And there could be so many more of these tiny oases. Gardens can fill more roles than just looking good: they can provide habitats for wildlife, absorb pollutants and reduce city temperatures – all we need to do is think a little more about what we plant.

01

Learn
Understand the bright side of shade

Embrace the shadows

Learning about shade, and understanding its potential benefits, can not only transform the places you garden, but also give you an appreciation (and hopefully love) for different light levels that can open up a whole new perspective on gardening and nature. Embracing the shadows rather than fighting them is key to creating a garden in shade.

This chapter explores the way in which plants adapt to and thrive in restricted light, and it explores the different types of shade you might come across, as well as the soil you might be gardening in. It essentially asks you to think about what your garden, balcony or windowsill has going for it. How much direct sunlight does it get? Does that light change significantly across different sections? Do you have clay or sandy soil? This knowledge can make a real difference to which plants will work best for you.

It always makes more sense (and will result in more successful planting) if you embrace the conditions you have and find plants that suit them, rather than spending a lot of money on enriching soil, banishing shade and installing irrigation systems. This may sound complicated, but it can simply boil down to knowing that you have clay soil and only get direct light in the morning – this gives you the basic conditions you need to bear in mind before looking for suitable plants.

Almost everyone has areas of shade in their outside spaces; it might come from a neighbouring tree, a nearby building, tall or dense shrubs, an overhanging balcony, a side return or another issue. Generally, we see this as a 'problem area', but it doesn't have to be that way.

Full sun is often thought of as ideal for gardens and plants, but in that bright light there's nowhere to hide. Many of the plants that can cope with lots of sun put huge amounts of energy into protecting themselves from the UV rays and heat that can damage their leaves, inhibit photosynthesis (and therefore growth) and increase transpiration (water loss). Full sun can also dry the earth and heat up the soil, creating less-than-ideal conditions for plants and other organisms to thrive.

Given our recurring summer droughts, shade is a vital resource that we should be creating more of wherever possible. As our weather becomes ever more extreme, we need to encourage shade into our gardens rather than trying to banish it – it's better for us, for wildlife and for the planet.

Providing more shade (or simply embracing the shade you have rather than expending energy on eradicating it) means less work for you and less input of valuable resources. Overall, it means watering less frequently and less stress on the plants. Shade provides shelter for insects and pollinators and protects us from the sun. Shady borders tend to look better for longer in the season, with less maintenance than a border in full sun. For example, while blooms may be a little smaller on shade plants they don't require as much deadheading, and the soil doesn't need as much weeding and mulching.

HOW TO CREATE MORE SHADE

Creating more shade is not a sacrifice in terms of gardening and if you want to introduce more shade to your space, consider planting deciduous trees; multi-stem specimens with delicate foliage work well in small spaces, providing an airy structure and dappled shade. You could also add a structure such as a pergola or gazebo and then swathe it in climbers.

In small gardens or yards, try adding plants with oversized foliage such as a gunnera or Chinese rice-paper plant 'Rex' (*Tetrapanax papyrifer* 'Rex') – both, at a pinch, could be grown in large containers as long as they are kept moist. Layering different sized plants can provide privacy, create inviting nooks and add depth and drama. Foliage has a big part to play in creating shade and often results

in the most lush and relaxing planting. You can play with different textures, tones and shapes, and most shades of green look better in low light.

If you have a lawn, think about reducing its size. Lawns are hard work to keep going: they need a lot of water and often require chemicals to keep them weed-free. Creating a smaller lawn is a good way to start making your garden more sustainable and introducing more shade. To do this, you could increase the size of your borders or you could plant into the lawn – a mixture of wild violet (*Viola odorata*), types of deadnettle (*Lamium*), wild strawberry (*Fragaria vesca*) and mind-your-own-business (*Soleirolia soleirolii*) would give an alternative lawn that is more biodiverse, lower maintenance and happy in lower light. It's mowable too.

SHADE IN URBAN AREAS

Nature can exist in abundance in cities, but we don't always notice it. Wild flowers that push through cracks and clamber over walls tell us that, despite being a hostile and often very shady environment, urban areas can be home to many more plants if we let them in. We shouldn't need to travel out of town to immerse ourselves in nature; there are so many municipal areas that could be home to vast areas of sustainable planting if only we gave it a try.

Perhaps surprisingly, cities and towns are important refuges for insect pollinators. Intensive farming (among other factors) has meant a drastic reduction in biodiversity across the UK, and urban areas have the ability to do more to help by providing foraging and nesting sites as well as food. Biodiversity in planting – that is, encouraging a wide range of different plants – is key to supporting these tiny but vital creatures. In the UK, there has been a move to reduce the frequency of mowing in many public spaces such as roadside verges, traffic islands and along railway lines. It's a great start in terms of

The oversized foliage of a Chinese rice-paper plant 'Rex' (*Tetrapanax papyrifer* 'Rex')

wildlife habitats and biodiversity, and is something we should continue campaigning for. But there's so much more that can be done.

Directly in our control are the many empty balconies and front gardens that could be covered in greenery and flowers, and be teeming with life. The luxury flats opposite my little plant shop Linda have wide, empty glass balconies that overhang each other: they are not easy places to garden, but with the right plants they could be verdant oases for residents to look out on and beautiful mini-gardens for passersby to enjoy from the street.

Urban areas are not accommodating environments for living things – plants, people, insects and animals – so the greener we can make our homes and surrounding areas the better the outcome for us all. Almost 50 per cent of urban green spaces in the UK are private gardens, so what we choose to do with them – and plant in them – can make a big difference to the local and wider environment. If every balcony or street corner had a garden on it, it would reduce our carbon footprint and potentially air pollution, it would make a difference to our view and our wellbeing, and it would encourage biodiversity and increase the ability of pollinators to move freely.

For many people, living in a city means limited square footage and no access to green space. If a city dweller does have outside space, it is commonly in the shadow of buildings. Balconies are often constructed in concrete or glass and at first glance they don't seem welcoming places for gardening. It's easy to give up once you've tried a few things that have not survived, but choosing the right plants is half the battle, and learning what you need to do to look after them is the other half.

Shade gardens really suit urban environments. Urban garden spaces often come with their own microclimates by virtue of walls and concrete (see page 42). These warm, sheltered conditions might allow us to plant tender, exotic plants that would otherwise suffer in a large, exposed garden. And green foliage, delicate flowers and movement of light across plants contrasts well with the hard materials and clean lines of urban architecture. More than that, these gardens can provide respite from city pressures – looking at and caring for plants can make a significant difference to our quality of life. Learning a plant's name and how to look after it is a simple but very effective way of reconnecting with nature.

Shade tolerance

A plant's ability to tolerate different levels of light – from full sun to deep shade – varies from species to species, plant to plant. Depending on various adaptations, a plant can either thrive in low light or suffer and eventually die. All plants need sunlight, but many plants have the ability to live and even germinate happily in shade, expending minimal energy and making full use of the nutrients and moisture found in shaded soil – it's these survivors that will bring your dark corners to life.

ADAPTING TO LOW LIGHT

Whatever the light conditions, plants need sunlight, water and carbon dioxide in order to create oxygen and sugars, which provide them with the energy they need to grow – this process is called photosynthesis. Water should be present in the soil, which can be drawn up through a plant's roots, and carbon dioxide is in the air. But providing the right amount of light is key to having a healthy plant that's able to photosynthesise efficiently and to grow and thrive.

Plants are capable of adapting their roots, stems and foliage to suit their environments. Shade-tolerant plants are those that have adapted to handle lower light intensities and still create enough food to survive. Due to the extra challenges, they are prone to being slow growing, but are more energy efficient; they photosynthesise more quickly in low light than plants in lots of sun. They also transpire (release water through their leaves) more slowly, meaning that they burn less sugar and conserve energy.

Plants contain a green pigment called chlorophyll which is contained in small structures, or organelles, called chloroplasts. Chlorophyll's main purpose is to harness the energy of sunlight, captured through the plants' leaves, to make glucose.

The dark green leaves of a castor oil plant
(*Fatsia japonica*)

Shade-tolerant plants can be a darker shade of green (compared to sun-lovers) due to higher chlorophyll levels and chloroplasts that are closer to the leaf surface in order to capture as much light as possible.

Another way shade-tolerant plants can adapt to a lack of light is by growing bigger, thinner leaves to better catch rays and photosynthesise effectively. Other adaptations include their shoots growing more quickly to reach for light, which results in longer internodes (the stem between leaf nodes).

In contrast, plants that need to survive in full sun have their own characteristics that help them to cope. Mediterranean plants, for example,

often have small-leaved foliage with limited surface area to reduce transpiration – think of plants such as rosemary and lavender, or even the spines of a cactus, which are actually modified leaves. They might also have leaves covered in very fine hairs which trap moisture, or silvery foliage to reflect the light.

SHAPE SHIFTING

Plants tend to react to a shortage of light in two ways: they tolerate it or they must battle it. The battlers are not the ones we want: in shade, these can become etiolated, which means their stems become elongated and weak as they reach for any available light. But sometimes there is a middle ground between 'tolerate' and 'battle' when a lack of light can result in a plant shape that perhaps isn't traditional, but is one you like. The pelargoniums I grow are more leggy, less bushy and produce fewer flowers than pelargoniums in full sun (because they are having to reach for light) and luckily I prefer them like that. I grow scented-leaf varieties – such as velvety, minty *P. tomentosum* or the glorious 'Attar of Roses' – as I'm more interested in their foliage than their flowers. Another example is my *Hydrangea paniculata* 'Limelight'. This is usually a bushy shrub that prefers full sun or partial shade; in my garden, with just a few hours of afternoon light, it's a much airier-looking plant, and again, I prefer it this way.

Assessing shade in your garden

Shade is created when sunlight is blocked by an object or an object is casting a shadow. Assessing it in your garden is best done in late spring and early summer (in the UK, this is May and June), as this is when we receive the most hours of light and the shadows are shortest.

There is a definite hierarchy when it comes to types of garden shade and almost all gardens have some shade. This section will help you understand what type of shade you have and its seasonal behaviour.

SEASONAL SHADE

The amount of shade a garden has will change according to the season and depend on how high the sun is and whether surrounding trees and plants still have their leaves.

You may find you only have a few hours of sun a day during winter, but summer gives you a good five hours across the middle (and hottest) part of the day.

The amount of shade may also change over time as trees and shrubs grow bigger, so keep an eye on seasonal changes over the years.

The sun's seasonal position

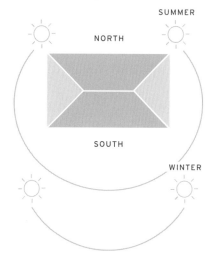

ASPECT

Before you start thinking about what you want to plant, work out how much light your garden gets depending on which way it faces. In the UK, May is a good month to do this, as leaves will be on the trees and the sun is getting higher, so you can see how the shadows fall.

Stand with your back to your home, but facing your garden or balcony: this is the direction your garden or balcony faces. So if you are facing south, then your garden or balcony is south-facing. This means the garden boundary opposite – which might be a fence, hedge, wall or balcony edge – is north-facing and will likely be in shade over the middle part of the day.

East-facing gardens (which will have a west-facing boundary) get most of their light in the morning, sometimes until midday, while west-facing spaces will get most of their light in the afternoon and evening. If you have a walled, west-facing garden, the brickwork will retain heat and radiate it back through the evening, offering a very sheltered microclimate.

North-facing gardens have very little direct light – perhaps some early morning sun and some sun last thing in the evening during the summer – but it is consistent and there aren't extremes, meaning that if you do find plants that work, they'll be happy!

So much of gardening is trial and error, so if you really like a plant and it can take some shade, try it no matter the aspect. Signs that a plant isn't receiving enough light are very pale, spindly stems and foliage, limited growth and small or no flowers. Don't be afraid to move a plant if it looks unhappy; some plants hate their roots being disturbed, but most are fine with it (though avoid moving them in summer or when flowering).

SHADES OF SHADE

Some types and combinations of shade are harder to work with than others. For example, a combination of full and dry shade found under a tree is trickiest, because the canopy blocks the light and the tree's roots dry out the soil. Moderate shade cast by a building can be more forgiving, as it can shift as the sun moves.

I've outlined different types of shade below based on the light available in midsummer, but you will always need to assess the specifics of your plot. These are not hard-and-fast rules, as there are so many variables, but they will give you a good idea of how to approach the shade in your space.

Light shade Five or six hours of direct sunlight at any time of day (over six hours constitutes full sun). This might be a solid block of sunlight across the middle part of the day when the sun is at its hottest, or it could be a good burst of light for a few hours in the morning and again in the afternoon.

Light shade can also describe indirect light that's available all day. I have almost no direct sunlight on my shop's courtyard, as it is surrounded by tall buildings, but the space has open access to the sky so it receives indirect light all day.

Filtered or dappled shade Five hours or more of indirect or diffused light. This could be sunlight passing through some kind of overhead structure, such as a plant-covered pergola, or coming through the delicate foliage of a deciduous tree, such as a birch or mimosa.

A multi-stem silver birch (*Betula pendula*) in dappled shade against a north-facing wall

Deep shade at the back of a walled garden, together with dappled shade at the front

Semi-shade / part shade / partial shade Between four and five hours of direct sunlight over a full day.

Moderate / medium shade Two to three hours of direct sunlight at any time of day apart from around midday, as this is when the sun is at its hottest and would constitute semi-shade.

Full shade / deep shade This means anything less than two hours of direct sunlight. It might be under some evergreen trees, a spot in a built-up area or a window box on a north-facing wall.

Damp shade Less of a problem in urban areas, damp shade is usually found alongside waterways (springs, rivers, natural ponds and so on) and often beneath the bases of trees that grow along them, but it can also present in poor-draining areas in your garden where the soil never dries out.

Dry shade This is usually found in rain shadows at the bases of walls or fences, where rain doesn't hit the ground. It can also be found underneath trees where the canopy blocks the sun and the trees' roots absorb a lot of moisture.

Assessing soil

Soil is a huge topic and is key to how successful your growing will be, so knowing your soil's composition is a vital place to start. All soil is a combination of inorganic (rocks) and organic (bacteria, plants, fungi, air and water) material.

Drainage and nutrients are the main factors you need to consider. Drainage – that is, the ability of water to travel easily down through the soil – depends on the size of the soil particles. Clay has much smaller particles than sand and therefore is less free-draining than sandy soils, which can leach nutrients. Clay soil tends to be more nutrient-rich compared to sandy soil.

Frequent warm, wet winters mean some soils (particularly clay) can become saturated with water and therefore become anaerobic (devoid of oxygen) leaving plant roots to rot in soggy soil. If your soil is dense or easily saturated, you can add horticultural grit for better drainage.

Saturated soil is prone to compaction, which is the collapse of soil structure due to foot traffic or some other form of compression. Compacted soil is hard to work and break down; plant roots won't be able to grow properly and earthworms won't be able to travel through it. Adding mulch and organic matter can improve the structure of your soil.

You can't change soil texture, but you can improve it. Everything in soil – be it the plants, invertebrates or fungi – need organic matter to survive. If you do want to improve your soil, adding an organic mulch once or twice a year will introduce nutrients and microorganisms that will break down your soil, suppress weeds and improve the drainage. The best time to do this is in April and again in autumn or early winter. You can find out a bit more about mulch on page 142.

If the soil in your garden doesn't suit the particular plants you're keen to grow, consider making use of pots and planters. You can fill them with specialised composts that are tailor-made for the needs of different plants.

DIFFERENT SOIL TYPES

You can go to great lengths to test your soil, but the simplest and quickest way is to feel it.

Dig out a section, at least 30cm deep, then squeeze a small amount of moist (not wet) soil in your hand. As a very general rule of thumb: if it falls apart immediately it is sandy; if it stays in a clump, it is clay; and if it's crumbly it is loam.

Another test you can do is to push some firm but pliable wire into the soil and see where it bends. Ideally it shouldn't bend until it is at least 30cm deep, less than this means the soil is very compacted.

These are the main types of soil:

Clay This is nutrient-rich but poor-draining. It can be heavy, hard to work and become compacted. This can lead to drainage problems if it becomes saturated with water, thereby reducing the amount of oxygen in the soil. London soil is often clay.

Silt This is free-draining, fairly rich in nutrients and easy to work, but it can still become compacted.

Chalk Usually stony, chalk soil has good drainage, but is not very fertile. It also tends to be more alkaline in its pH, which is important to consider when choosing your plants.

Sand With excellent drainage, sandy soil warms up quickly and is easy to work, but it has fewer nutrients than other soils as they get washed away.

Loam This has a roughly even mix of clay, sand and silt meaning it has good drainage, lots of nutrients and is easy to work – it is the ideal soil type.

Top A handful of clay soil from my garden
Bottom Raised beds or planters can be filled with specialised composts

Shade gardens /
Garden Museum

Design Dan Pearson Studio
Head gardener Matt Collins

The cloistered courtyard garden in London's Garden Museum, together with the woodland planting between the museum's cafe and the street, has long been one of my favourite green spaces accessible to the public.

It receives strong, early spring sun and then diffused light throughout the rest of the growing season; its sheltered position creates a microclimate that allows tender perennials and horticultural curiosities to flourish.

It was looking particularly herbaceous when I visited one August after a long, wet and not particularly sunny summer. The woodland planting was glorious with white wood asters (*Eurybia divaricata*) and Japanese anemones (*A. × hybrida*) glowing through grasses and shrubs. Designed by Dan Pearson Studio, it is now looked after by head gardener Matt Collins, who told me about the evolving space.

27

'Because they're on show 360-odd days a year, plants have to work very hard in the courtyard, bringing something dynamic and interesting to the space and offering a long season of interest. Australian violets (Viola hederacea) begin flowering in spring and continue right up to the first frost, while the Japanese shield ferns (Dryopteris erythrosora) change colour through the seasons, unfurling rust-orange before shifting to green.

There's a kind of stoic energy to shade gardens that I really enjoy; the surprise and respect you feel encountering the quiet existence of plants thriving in what can sometimes seem like forgotten or overlooked spaces. They can be profoundly restful, comforting and inspiring environments, places of escape and refuge.'

02

Plan
Shape your space with intention and purpose

On first appearance, a dark corner or 'tricky' spot might appear gloomy and unwelcoming, but when filled with foliage that shady area can become calm, inviting and restful. Understanding the conditions of your garden – the light and soil type for example – is a key place to start and this is covered in the Learn chapter (see page 10). This chapter builds on that knowledge and looks at different types of space and the various conditions you need to consider before you invest in (often expensive) plants. Once you have a handle on your plot, move on to think about structure, form and colour throughout the year. You can note down plants and combinations you like and work from there to create a planting plan.

What is your plot like?

Get to know your garden, balcony, courtyard or even windowsill and it will give you more options when it comes to planting. Here I've outlined different types of shady areas, together with things to think about, design advice and inspiration on how to garden these spaces.

URBAN GARDENS AND COURTYARDS

City gardens and courtyards often have high walls or fences surrounding them and are frequently overlooked. Boundaries are much more apparent when you only have a small space, so working to disguise these can help give the impression of a larger area and also adds privacy.

Create depth Layering plants with varying shades of green, leaf textures and heights and forms can create a sense of depth.

The combination of evergreen star jasmine (*Trachelospermum jasminoides*), *Hydrangea paniculata* 'Limelight' and Japanese anemones (*A. × hybrida*) is hardworking and lovely. For a more woodland vibe try the soft shield fern (*Polystichum setiferum*), *Brunnera macrophylla* 'Jack Frost' and snowy wood-rush (*Luzula nivea*).

Different foliage heights and forms create a
layered patchwork of planting

Another idea is to add patches
of lighter foliage at the end of a
courtyard, garden or under a tree,
such as a silvery deadnettle (*Lamium*)
or pale green hosta. This adds depth
and can emulate sunlight through
trees. A mirror tucked in a corner,
semi-obscured by foliage, can reflect
back other planting and light for a
similar effect.

A sense of depth often relies on not
seeing the whole garden at a glance,
but this can be very difficult to achieve
in a tiny space. Bi-fold doors that
expose the whole garden at once can
take away so much intrigue, whereas
double-doors opening onto a well-
planted side return or yard can offer a
more engaging journey into a garden.

A mirror at the back of a courtyard reflects light
and planting

A small multi-stem tree as a focal
point, strategically positioned, provides
an airier view and has the added
benefit of providing structure and
winter interest.

Use backdrops Brick or stone walls
that might initially seem stark or
enclosing can provide a beautiful
backdrop to plants, while fences can be
painted in a dark colour (such as a slate
grey or black), which works well with

green foliage and white flowers. For maximum coverage of a wall or fence – or to raise it for privacy – add a wide slatted trellis that will support climbers but still let in shafts of light.

Adopt a landscape Borrowed landscapes are something much discussed when working in bigger gardens, but can work equally well in a small, built-up area. If your neighbour has a beautiful acer or fig tree that overhangs your garden, embrace this as part of your own space, and even repeat the plant or colour in your garden if you have the room. I get a lot of comments about the evergreen honeysuckle that pours down one wall of the Linda courtyard, but it's not ours; it's actually planted in the garden next door and is just a welcome visitor (pictured on page 37).

Employ pots and planters A container garden is a brilliant way of transforming the hard surfaces of an urban courtyard (see page 59 for more on this). The courtyard of my plant shop is roughly 5m x 5m, so space is at a premium (see page 152). Many of the plants sit on wide, staggered shelving made from scaffolding planks installed against one wall. Large pots and planters are at the back, smaller ones at the front. Many more are balanced on old crates, wooden chairs and found blocks of wood. A couple of 1m tree ferns (*Dicksonia antarctica*) sit in big pots on stools, their long, friendly fronds waving over the heads of the other plants. Plus there's the borrowed landscape of honeysuckle. All together, this gives a feeling of depth and interest that belies the size of the space. Because the plants are mostly stock for the shop and are in small pots, it takes a bit of maintenance to keep it from looking messy, but if it wasn't a shop I would add several more large planters full of perennials and evergreen ferns to the shelves and use the rest for seating.

SHADE FROM A NEIGHBOURING TREE

It can be frustrating if deep shade is being created by a neighbouring garden, but there are ways to improve the situation. If a neighbour's tree overshadows most of your garden and light is very restricted, you can ask them to cut it back. It's often a sensitive matter, particularly if the tree is providing privacy, so be prepared for the possibility that your suggestion is unwelcome. One idea you can suggest to the neighbour is 'crown lifting' (which is the process of removing some of the lower branches), or thinning the tree's branches, both of which can increase the amount of light beneath a tree significantly. Legally, though, you can cut down anything that's on your side – though you do have to return the wood to the neighbour. If the tree is very established, you should get a tree surgeon to do this to preserve the shape and health of the tree.

Climbing hydrangea (*H. petiolaris*) and chocolate vine (*Akebia quinata*)

A pelargonium on a shelf made from a scaffolding plank

SIDE RETURNS

Many terraced houses in the UK have side returns – the long alley or corridor-like strip that runs down one side of the building – and these are typically used for storage, dumping things you don't want and fencing off the view from the neighbours. Often a side return ends up being swallowed into a glass kitchen extension. Looking out onto a lush wall of planting is an option that rarely seems to be considered.

These spaces are usually sheltered and the perfect place for some jungle foliage or woodland planting. You can dig a narrow bed or place a series of large containers or pots along the wall or fence to create something magical.

Climbers such as a sausage vine (*Holboellia coriacea*), climbing hydrangea (*H. petiolaris*) or a common ivy (*Hedera helix*) are great for creating a background of greenery.

Exotic plants such as giant rhubarb (*Gunnera manicata*) or Chinese rice-paper plant 'Rex' (*Tetrapanax papyrifer* 'Rex') bring drama and can work if placed at the lightest end of a dark passage. These can work in very large pots, but be aware that they will need a lot of watering.

I'm not the biggest fan of bamboo, but black bamboo (*Phyllostachys nigra*) in deep containers can be regularly thinned out to expose the beautiful stems, and together with

some native ferns would give privacy and a lovely soft, dynamic green view – try underplanting with deer fern (*Blechnum spicant*) or hart's tongue fern (*Asplenium scolopendrium*).

If you are only gardening with pots, bear in mind that groups of plants in a few big pots can feel calming whereas lots of different plants in small pots will feel cluttered. You can layer pots by adding a few smaller, different sized containers in front of the very largest one and fill these with ferns and tiarellas to create more depth and attract pollinators.

STEPS, LIGHTWELLS AND OTHER AWKWARD SPACES

Side returns aren't the only awkward spaces you might be living with. I have a lower basement lightwell that receives a few hours of morning sun and a lot of litter that blows in from the street. I also have a set of dank concrete steps leading down to the same lower basement level which receives a couple of hours of late-afternoon and early evening sun (pictured opposite top right and bottom left and right).

I have filled the lightwell with an array of pots and planters and planted a couple of smallish tree ferns (*Dicksonia antarctica*), a golden hop (*Humulus lupulus* 'Aureus'), a mixture of ferns (including evergreen maidenhair and soft shield), rose 'Mme Alfred

Carrière' (which has yet to flower in all honesty, but I live in hope) and some giant hogweed (*Heracleum sphondylium* 'Pink Cloud'). Bulbs pop up in the spring and maidenhair vine (*Muehlenbeckia complexa*) climbs over the tops of the pots. Self-seeded yellow corydalis (*C. lutea*) gives a bright pop of colour around the top and softens the concrete pavement.

The steps are now home to a varied assortment of large ferns, several different cultivars of Solomon's seal (*Polygonatum* × *hybridum*) and two climbers: a sausage vine (*Holboellia coriacea*) and a climbing hydrangea (*H. petiolaris*). There is barely any space on the steps themselves for access, but we rarely use them, and more is definitely more in this case.

The plants in both areas are a mixture of evergreen and deciduous and they are all in pots or large planters, but because they receive such limited light they don't require nearly as much watering as planters in the sun.

FRONT GARDENS

South-facing back gardens are often considered the ideal, but investing in a property with a sunny back garden means that the front garden is north-facing and somewhat shady. If planted at all, they tend to be palmed-off with some evergreen shrubs and some bedding plants, but more often than not they are given up on altogether and paved over or converted into a car-parking space. An RHS report from 2020 found that introducing plants to your front garden could significantly reduce stress, which makes sense, as you have to pass by them every day on your way in and out of the house.

A multi-stem Himalayan birch (*Betula utilis*), a few mounds of pheasant's tail grass (*Anemanthele lessoniana*) and scented sweet box (*Sarcococca confusa*) interplanted with snowdrops (*Galanthus*), hellebores, astrantias and Japanese anemones (*A. × hybrida*) will give you lovely, low-maintenance planting and interest all year round.

If you've turned your front garden into a parking space, add some generous planters to soften the edges or consider a pollution-tolerant, wildlife-friendly hedge such as hawthorn (*Crataegus*) mixed up with quince (*Chaenomeles speciosa*), hazel (*Corylus*) and spindle (*Euonymus europaeus*). These can be underplanted with deadnettle (*Lamium*), garlic mustard (*Alliaria petiolata*) and hedge nettle (*Stachys sylvatica*) to provide even more for benefits to wildlife.

PLANTING UNDER TREES
Underplanting large trees or a dense block of evergreens is always tricky. The tree roots tend to make the soil very dry as they absorb a lot of moisture. Tree roots are also delicate

and many are often close to the surface and need to be able to breathe. Putting a lot of soil on top of these roots to plant into is not going to do the tree any good and can deprive it of oxygen. Rain shadows (areas that receive no rain) that crop up alongside house or garden walls can be equally tricky to plant and the options listed below apply to these areas too. If none of the suggestions is suitable, turn the space over to practical purposes – use it to store logs, pots, bins or create a compost heap.

Into the ground If you are planting under a tree, add a small quantity of soil (2–5cm maximum) and choose small plants that don't have deep roots (preferably plug plants or those in 9cm pots). Spring bulbs are great if the tree is deciduous and shallow-rooted. Mat-forming ground cover such as lesser periwinkle (*Vinca minor*), wood sorrels (*Oxalis*), blue violets (*Viola sororia* 'Freckles') or wild strawberries (*Fragaria vesca*) work well in really tough areas. Adding a bench makes a good focal point, as well as a pleasant shady spot to sit in.

Alternative options It's worth considering other options to planting in the ground, especially if you have shade from dense evergreens or hedging such Leyland cypress (× *Cuprocyparis leylandii*), which creates very dusty, dry ground beneath it. If you have the room, use a long planter, being careful of any tree roots and placing it on raised feet or bricks so that air can circulate underneath. Fill with hardy ferns like hart's tongue fern (*Asplenium scolopendrium*) and Japanese shield fern (*Dryopteris erythrosora*), and mix with epimediums and astrantias. If you have a suitable tree, you could grow a climber that can scramble up it, a Virginia creeper (*Parthenocissus quinquefolia*) would work well here; Chinese Virginia creeper (*P. henryana*) is a particularly nice speices with distinctive foliage.

Mixed planting in a walled garden including *Salvia guaranitica*, soft shield fern (*Polystichum setiferum*) and foxgloves (*Digitalis*)

MICROCLIMATES

Microclimates are climates specific to small areas. The most familiar one might be the microclimate of an urban area compared to its rural surroundings. On average, urban areas are a couple of degrees Celsius warmer and a little bit wetter than rural areas. Within urban environments, tall buildings can often reduce wind speeds and walls provide shelter, absorb heat and reflect it back out at night, which allows more tender plants to survive. But you can also find smaller areas within any garden that have their own microclimates.

You might notice the soil in south-facing beds dries out and cracks or the soil in a corner of a north-facing bed may never completely dry out. Or you may get rain shadows. These can form at the base of walls or under trees and occur when an area receives no rain because of an obstruction or shelter. Rain tends to fall at an angle, often from the south-west in the UK, meaning that the north and east sides of a house can get a narrow strip of ground at their base that remains dry.

No matter how small your plot, it always takes time to notice these small differences. Choosing plants that enjoy the same conditions means that they are more likely to survive in these spots. And if we can find plants that don't compete with each other, we're winning. It means that they will happily co-exist and we will have less work to do in terms of watering or weeding.

MULTIPLE ASPECTS IN ONE SPACE

Even a small garden can have very different conditions within it. It may be that you have one bed in full sun and another in deep shade, which can make your planting feel disjointed. If you have very different aspects, repeating plants that are tolerant of a wide variety of light conditions helps to pull the space together.

I have Welsh poppies (*Meconopsis cambrica*) that have self-seeded across my garden including in pots and cracks in the bricks; I love them and they really tie different parts of the garden together. Astrantias, euphorbias, erigeron, hostas, Scots lovage (*Ligusticum scoticum*), pheasant's tail grass (*Anemanthele lessoniana*), viburnums and hydrangeas can grow in varying degrees of light and shade and can be planted around the garden to provide continuity. They may behave differently depending on how many hours of sunlight they get – for example, lower light may result in fewer flowers and an airier structure in a plant like a hydrangea, or it could mean less variation in leaf colour for a grass like pheasant's tail – but these differences can add to the planting.

WIND AND EXPOSED SPACES

The higher up your garden and the more exposed your space, the more

Mixed foliage including hart's tongue fern (*Asplenium scolopendrium*), lady's mantle (*Alchemilla mollis*), maidenhair vine (*Muehlenbeckia complexa*) and Scots lovage (*Ligusticum scoticum*)

wind becomes a factor. If you have a sixteenth storey balcony, you need flexible plants that will move with the wind, not snap at the first sign of a breeze. Wind is not just a problem for balconies, soil in windy sites (whether in planters or the ground) can also dry out faster than sheltered ones, so you preferably need to look for plants that can tolerate this. Many grasses are suitable on both fronts and look lovely planted with hardy geraniums, Mexican fleabane (*Erigeron karvinskianus*) and lady's mantle (*Alchemilla mollis*). If there's something you really want, it's worth looking out for new cultivars as you can sometimes find a shorter version of a favourite plant that may withstand an exposed site.

The simplest way to diffuse the wind is with foliage or a trellis; this is better than blocking it with something solid. It's often for this reason I include grasses in my planters, plus they provide height and screening and movement, and bring a soft, naturalistic look to the planting.

Snowy wood-rush (*Luzula nivea*) is my favourite shade-loving grass: it's not showy, it's hardworking and tough, it can take dry shade and it works with almost everything. Japanese forest grass (*Hakonechloa macra*) is a deciduous grass and adds some glamour when planted en masse, particularly in large pots

Planters containing grasses and hardy ferns can diffuse wind on an exposed balcony

or beneath trees, though it prefers a bit more light to snowy wood-rush. Pheasant's tail grass (*Anemanthele lessoniana*) is another very useful one: it is evergreen and its foliage can be shot with autumnal hues depending on the amount of light it gets. None of these becomes huge, and all work in planters or pots.

Planning your planting

I'm as guilty as anybody when it comes to returning from a nursery having been totally seduced by a plant that I have no room for and doesn't work with the ones in my garden. That's fundamental to how I learnt to garden – moving on from mistakes, embracing and then repeating surprise successes and trying to slow down and resist the desire for instant impact. But if you're not careful, you end up with a completely random selection of lots of different plants with different needs, which is not a recipe for a harmonious planting plan or happy plants. It's easy to focus on the summer flowerers, but don't forget spring bulbs and early flowering plants are essential for spring, while foliage colour, distinctive barks and evergreens are very useful for autumn and winter.

I'm not a believer in people having 'green fingers' – I think you have to just make a start. No plant is self-sufficient, they all need some care: they need air around their roots, nutrients in the soil, moisture, warmth and light. Planning helps, but so does paying close attention. I'm more of a trier than a planner, but I have trained myself over time to be more considered in my approach and I hope the planning tips in the following pages also help you to create a plan before facing the temptations of a good nursery.

Gardening is a lot to do with patience, so when you're in planning mode try to resist the temptation to cram every space full of plants – you need time to watch things unfurl, spread out and adjust to their new home. Ground-cover plants will gradually fill any gaps for you (see page 93).

If you have planted something that's not doing well, check again on the conditions it likes, watch it for a while, move it if necessary and watch again to see if it likes its new home better. Most plants are more resilient than you think and will thank you for being put in a more suitable spot. My mistakes often get planted into pots and moved around until I work out if there's a way to keep them – they can get added to a cluster of other pots or put on a windowsill or doorstep. Ultimately, if the plant doesn't work anywhere, it gets rehomed.

KNOW YOUR PLANT

Putting the right plants in the right environment is the first step towards encouraging them to live. It also does a lot for your gardening confidence; having plants continually die on you is never fun. This is not to say there isn't room for experimentation – lots of plants that, according to their labels, require full sun can be very happy in a shadier spot.

Plant labels usually only give broad brushstrokes in terms of what a plant needs to survive. A simple sun symbol that's half-shaded to indicate how much light the plant can tolerate rarely tells the whole story. Nothing will survive with no light at all and 'light shade' can be very different to 'part shade', though they still might have the same half-shade symbol. It's always worth a quick google to find out more details on what the plant might like.

In the UK, the RHS and Beth Chatto Gardens are both excellent resources for this. You also might have noticed the same plant growing in a friend's garden, so you could find out more about the conditions they have.

FIND IDEAS IN NATURE

When we look at plants growing in the wild, one thing that's apparent is the lack of bare soil. Plants in the wild do not grow in the same way as plants in your garden because they work with each other as communities and have adapted to their environment, performing different roles and therefore requiring little maintenance. Conversely, we work hard in our gardens to keep the plants we want alive and the plants we don't want weeded out.

A patch of weeds in a disused spot of ground can provide inspiration for your garden if you look closely. We can approximate these natural plant communities to give a harmonious, diverse and lower-maintenance garden. The popularity of meadow-style planting signals our desire to be more connected to nature and creating small wildernesses in the city softens our view and slows us down.

You can take note of the natural life cycle of plants in the wild and let your gardening follow suit. For example, many woodland shade plants such as snowdrops (*Galanthus*), wood anemones (*A. nemorosa*) and wild violet (*Viola odorata*) flower from late winter to spring. This is when the trees are bare of leaves, allowing these plants to make the most of the early light and work quickly to grow flowers, attract pollinators and set seed before the leaves return to the branches. Foliage then takes over from these early flowerers, providing good ground cover for the rest of the year: brunnera, wood spurge (*Euphorbia amygdaloides*) and sweet woodruff (*Galium odoratum*) are good examples of this. Midsummer is more about foliage, but astrantias, white wood aster (*Eurybia divaricata*), hydrangeas and thalictrums are all good later-summer flowerers.

CONSIDER WILDLIFE

It's becoming increasingly vital to think about whether the plants you're considering will have any benefits for wildlife – this planet's fellow inhabitants need our help to survive.

Hardy geranium

Chinese meadow rue (*Thalictrum delavayi*)

A common misconception is that shade is only about foliage and evergreens, but there are lots of beautiful pollinator-friendly flowering shrubs, perennials and bulbs that can bring colour to the darkest corners, drawing you and the wildlife in.

The perception of our gardens as individual plots of land to be tamed is changing as the climate emergency has highlighted the essential role wildlife plays in our ecosystem. Understanding that these private spaces form a small part of a larger environment can help you choose plants that will encourage more wildlife into the garden.

Reducing mowing, leaving some of your garden to grow a little wilder,

creating ponds for frogs and toads and planting nectar-rich plants can all be included in shade gardens.

A lot of shade-tolerant plants are excellent sources of food for a wide variety of pollinators. In the early part of the year, from January to May, hellebores, bleeding heart (*Lamprocapnos spectabilis*), brunnera, Solomon's seal (*Polygonatum × hybridum*) and lungwort (*Pulmonaria*) will be flowering. In a sheltered spot, honesty (*Lunaria*), hydrangea, hardy geraniums, Chinese meadow rue (*Thalictrum delavayi*), Japanese anemones (*A. × hybrida*) and astrantias can flower all the way to November.

Solitary bees (these are bees that don't live in a hive and don't produce honey)

are important pollinators and certain bees, such as carpenter bees, actually prefer to build their nests in the shade, while almost all bees need shelter from the sun at various times. If you have a lot of dry shade beneath trees, adding nectar-rich, drought-tolerant plants as ground cover – such as lungwort (*Pulmonaria*), sweet woodruff (*Galium odoratum*) and hardy geraniums – is good for this. A small pile of logs can provide a lot of food, shelter and nesting areas.

Window boxes can also be great for pollinators, providing a patchwork of nectar-rich pit stops in otherwise barren places. Mixing mint, deadnettle (*Lamium*), heuchera, tiarella, Scots lovage (*Ligusticum scoticum*) and Mexican fleabane (*Erigeron karvinskianus*) will make beautiful, fragrant, free-flowering containers and the pollinators will be very grateful.

It's worth remembering that many pollinators prefer single, open flowers. The more cultivated a plant is – especially those with double flowers – the less pollen or nectar they tend to have. They don't need to be big either, tiny flowers can hold a lot of pollen: herb Robert (*Geranium robertianum*) and ivy-leaved toadflax (*Cymbalaria muralis*) are really pretty and have small flowers. You can grow them in pots or borders, and they'll self-seed in brickwork cracks, softening hard surfaces at the same time as

Above Ivy-leaved toadflax (*Cymbalaria muralis*)
Opposite Lenten rose (*Helleborus orientalis*)

providing a good source of food for smaller pollinators. Solitary bees like masonry bees that nest in the ground or in walls find these plants especially useful. If you have some space add water. Even a very small shallow dish with planting around it can add something tranquil, and it is also great for wildlife. I have a Corten steel bowl with hardy geraniums planted around three quarters of the perimeter, which provides a bit of shelter for the birds that like to use the water for a bath.

LOOK TO YOUR NEIGHBOURS

A simple way of working out what might thrive in your garden is to look around and see what grows well in similar environments. Think of creating

a garden as a collaboration with what is already around you, rather than changing the existing conditions, and you will have more chance of success. Species that thrive locally are always a good indication of plants that will survive in your soil, but look particularly to those that grow in similar light conditions. It might be as straightforward as checking your neighbour's patch over the fence or the front garden opposite for inspiration.

THE 'NATIVE' QUESTION

There is a lot of discussion around what constitutes a 'native' plant and a lot of language around this subject is problematic – 'non-native', 'alien', 'invasive' – so I find it easier to work with the environment I'm in and concentrate on the conditions a plant likes when I'm choosing the planting. Many plants considered to be native in our gardens were brought here from other countries, often as a result of colonisation and in order to make money for those who took them. Separated from their home and sold as decorative plants, their original names and culinary or medicinal uses are often forgotten. Landscapes and climates change, plants that thrived in this country at one time may no longer be as suitable as a plant that originated elsewhere and has become naturalised.

We have warmer, wetter winters and dryer, hotter summers than we did fifty years ago. Diversity is more important.

SIZE MATTERS

The final height and width of a plant is a crucial thing to consider when planning which plants will go together and how you might position them. If you have a small space, you may not want a castor oil plant (*Fatsia japonica*) that can grow to 4m in height, or a gunnera, whose foliage can reach more than 2m in width – but then again, you might if you are going for a jungly, enclosed feel.

If you are planting a roof terrace or balcony, there may be weight restrictions to consider too – large planters full of soil are incredibly heavy, even more so when wet, so check any limitations on weight before you start planting.

And no matter how tempting it might be to fill up your garden with plants immediately, you need to give them room to grow. Check the labels – if a plant will reach its full size in two to three years' time, then you need to account for that. At the same time, leaving lots of space between plants just encourages weeds and soil degradation.

Filling in the gaps As well as planting ground-cover plants, you can sow annuals in the gaps – they are called 'annuals' because they grow, flower and set seed in one year, so they are fast growing then they disappear. Some of my favourite annuals to grow are salad leaves, which love a bit of shade, as do the herbs coriander, chervil and parsley – if you leave these to flower they will look very pretty. Welsh poppies (*Meconopsis cambrica*) are brilliant at seeding themselves about and are easy to pull out if you end up with too many. Dotted between your other plants, these sorts of plantings will knit the scheme together until your perennials reach their full size.

STRUCTURE AND FORM

When planning which plants will go together, I always aim for a variety of heights, shapes and shades of foliage, as these provide a great backdrop for more delicate flowers as well as depth and interest.

The use of evergreens Typically evergreens provide structure, which is crucial to a garden's design and is especially important over winter when there's not much else going on. However, I love watching my garden come to life in spring, bursting from virtually nothing, and I prefer to use the skeletons of deciduous multi-stem shrubs, grasses, seedheads and faded hydrangea flowers for my structure.

Borders and edging These are important, especially if you are planning more naturalistic planting.

Clean lines, even if it's just a mown or mulched path within a larger space, or Corten edging or brickwork in a small courtyard, can frame the planting and make it look intentional rather than haphazard. Strategically placed planters or focal point can also do this.

Repetition is key Even in a small space, repetition helps tie planting schemes together. You could choose grasses like grey sedge (*Carex divulsa*) or pheasant's tail grass (*Anemanthele lessoniana*) to weave through your planting or punctuate beds with an evergreen fern such as Japanese lace fern (*Polystichum polyblepharum*). Lighter foliage, such as a silver-leaved deadnettle (*Lamium*) or an acid-green acer, can lead your eye through the garden or along a balcony. Repetition doesn't just mean dotting the same

plant about, it also means repeating a group of plants for form, foliage colour and height that travels through the garden. For example, the soft ferny foliage of sweet cicely (*Myrrhis odorata*) planted with fringe cups (*Tellima grandiflora*), snowy wood-rush (*Luzula nivea*) and evergreen Korean rock ferns (*Polystichum tsussimense*) will work well repeated through a border (and equally well in a large planter). Rather than thinking of placing one plant in one space, think about working with several plants together and consider ground cover, mounded shapes and tall spires.

Height order vs view Tallest at the back, shortest in the front is the traditional method of planting, but that doesn't necessarily work if you can see the planting from both sides, so consider your garden design carefully. You can always play with this height order by adding 'see-through' plants in the middle, such as Chinese meadow rue (*Thalictrum delavayi*), which has the most beautiful, fern-like foliage and sprays of delicate flowers on tall stems, or valerian, with its clusters of pinkish-white flowers – both will allow you to peer through to the plants behind.

This arrangement of 'tallest at the back' is also tricky for a window box, which may look lovely to passersby on the street, but needs to work from the inside as well. I always make sure I plant plenty of bulbs on the nearest

Quaking grass (*Briza media*) and snowy wood-rush (*Luzula nivea*)

Evergreen ferns and the foliage of hellebores are a lovely and useful combination that can be repeated

The textures of white wood aster (*Eurybia divaricata*), Japanese forest grass (*Hakonechloa macra*) and Lenten rose (*Helleborus orientalis*)

Plant window boxes so they look good from the inside and out

side to the window and I add a couple of interesting plants so there's something going on from all sides. At the moment, I have some bladder campion (*Silene vulgaris*) coming up – it's not an example of 'right plant, right place', but I planted them last year as an experiment and they were beautiful, gangly and sprawled into the room when I opened the window. You couldn't see them from the street, but I could see them while having breakfast, which is great for me.

FLOWERS

While you won't be arranging large vases of dahlias cut from the garden, you can have beautiful plants flowering successively so there is something

beautiful in the garden (and potentially the vase) almost all year round.

Good examples of early flowering perennials include hellebores, fringe cups (*Tellima grandiflora*) and bleeding heart (*Lamprocapnos spectabilis*), as well as snowdrops (*Galanthus*), muscari and narcissi. In early summer, look to deadnettle (*Lamium*), lungwort (*Pulmonaria*), tiarellas, foxgloves (*Digitalis*), red campion (*Silene dioica*), heucheras and hardy geraniums. And for late summer to autumn, baneberry (*Actaea*), astilbe, Japanese anemone (*A. × hybrida*), persicaria and hydrangea can take over. A lot of the flowers I just listed are smaller and

more delicate in colour and shape than sun-loving perennials – so we're talking posies rather than full-on bouquets – but it's this delicacy and size that makes them so special.

FOLIAGE COLOUR

Try to include as wide a range of foliage as possible when choosing your plants, as that's what will give your planting definition. Variegated foliage is not the most fashionable, but it can provide invaluable contrast – there is a variegated wild strawberry (*Fragaria vesca*) cultivar in Arnold Circus that pops out at me every time I pass it.

Variegated or silver foliage can create areas of light, *Brunnera macrophylla* 'Jack Frost' or *Lamium maculatum* 'White Nancy' are both hardworking, easy to find and really lift a dark corner. In the same way, the combination of the intensely dark-leaved *Heuchera* 'Obsidian' with the silvery fronds of a Japanese painted fern (*Athyrium niponicum* var. *pictum*), and *Persicaria runcinata* 'Purple Fantasy' can create a strong pop of colour that breaks up the green. Similarly, another dark heuchera, 'Palace Purple', works well with the structural foliage of *Hosta* 'Devon's Green'.

Above Japanese painted fern (*Athyrium niponicum* var. *pictum*) **Opposite** A range of colourful foliage including *Heuchera* 'Obsidian' among different ferns

Container gardening

Planting in containers is not only a really useful way of moving plants around the garden (to change the feel or to follow seasonal light changes), but it also means you can take the plants with you if you move. This makes particular sense if you are renting your home and don't want to buy and care for plants only to leave them behind. It was a wrench to leave the decidedly unglamorous raised car-park bed which was my first garden, especially knowing it was unlikely to be looked after once I'd moved.

Container gardening also means you can grow things that like specific conditions or soils that wouldn't necessarily work in your garden beds. I grow all my scented pelargoniums in pots; they prefer free-draining soil, and I move them around to the sunniest spots and bring them indoors over winter.

Container gardening needn't be high maintenance, but remember the pots are reliant on you for watering and food — the nutrients in the soil are finite (see page 140 for more on fertilisers) so choose a good, peat-free, nutrient-rich compost. I usually add a good couple of handfuls of horticultural grit or sand to the soil to increase drainage, more if I'm planting herbs or pelargoniums, as these don't like wet soil. You can also add perlite or vermiculite: these mediums are light, water-retentive and improve drainage, so are particularly useful for hanging baskets or smaller pots which are prone to drying out quickly.

Make sure your container has drainage holes — if it doesn't, you can drill them in or put in a smaller plastic pot with drainage holes. If you do the latter, make sure the inner pot is slightly raised up so it doesn't end up sitting in water. Add some crocks (broken bits of terracotta pots) or stones to the bottom of the pot to help prevent the compost becoming water-logged.

Container sizes I always encourage the use of big, deep containers for planting. Traditional window boxes are often shallow because they are not designed for plants to grow in them for more than one season; they are designed to hold a series of bedding plants that give an immediate pop of colour and which can be dug out and replaced a couple of times a year. Bedding plants tend not to be insect-friendly, are intensively farmed and require huge amounts of energy to grow. Using larger, deeper containers allows you to plant a wider variety of plants with good seasonal interest and the chance to come back each year.

If you just have a windowsill, get the deepest, largest container you can fit on it. A small box – say, 60cm long and 30cm deep and wide – would suit a mixture of spring bulbs (muscari or wood anemones are perfect), a small evergreen fern such as a Korean rock fern (*Polystichum tsussimense*) and a couple of flowering perennials, such as a hardy geranium or heuchera. There will be something going on for most of the year.

Larger containers allow plants more room to grow and expand their roots, but that does make them heavy and hard to move. Unless you are planting a tree or large shrub, you can place something else at the bottom of the pot

(rather than compost) so that it is not so heavy to lift or expensive to fill. The two things I use the most are broken up polystyrene packaging and upside-down plastic plant pots.

Container shapes Using pots of different heights with different foliage plants in each gives a layered, lush feel and is far more effective than rows of same-height pots. Sometimes just one pot in a corner planted with three different plants of contrasting foliage is all it takes to soften a space.

Round pots look lovely in a cluster and give a softer look compared to rectangular or square planters, but they can take up more room. Straight lines

Above Large planters make an impact **Opposite** *Astrantia* 'Shaggy', *Hosta* 'Devon's Geen' and maidenhair vine (*Muehlenbeckia complexa*) form a good combination for a pot

tend to look more formal, but can be softened by foliage. It's better to stick to one or the other shape, as it's not always easy to arrange organic and rigid shapes together.

Container materials You can plant in practically anything from a traditional terracotta pot to an enamel tin bath as long as it has drainage holes. In general I prefer to keep things simple so that the plants are the ones that shine, although there's nothing wrong with having a beautiful statement planter as a focal point. Meyer's lemon (*Citrus × limon* 'Meyer') trees in large pots are underplanted with violets and repeated through the Garden Museum's cloistered garden (see page 29).

For large planters, galvanised steel, stone, concrete or a composite material like polystone work well. If you have room for a large collection of containers, you can mix and match materials, but be careful that it doesn't look too busy. Terracotta is always popular, but tends to look better when it is aged (and large vintage terracotta pots are not cheap!). Terracotta is a very porous material, which means air and moisture can escape. This helps avoid root rot but it also means you have to water the plant more frequently as the soil dries out faster, especially in hot weather. Glazed pots avoid this problem but can look a bit shiny and don't have the aesthetic warmth of a baked terracotta pot.

Plastic pots are cheaper, lighter and keep the moisture in but they don't look that nice and, crucially, aren't recyclable. However, an oversized, black plastic planter from a garden centre is a very cost-effective way of planting a statement or over-sized plant – it will last for years and can be disguised with other pots in front of it.

Window boxes A planter on your sill is an excellent way to be close to small, seasonal changes, and caring for window boxes was one of the ways I was seduced into gardening on a larger scale. Watching the trees change colour or burst into blossom is something most of us understand and appreciate, but noticing the tip of a snowdrop you planted a few months previously start to work its way through the soil is incredibly satisfying and encourages

A large and striking pot planted with a beautiful hosta makes a good focal point

Indian valerian (*Valeriana jatamansi*) in a worn terracotta pot can be all you need for impact

you to notice the less conspicuous unfurling of leaves you might otherwise have missed.

Window boxes are usually a manageable size and often at a height that means you won't have to bend down to see what's growing in them. They are perfect for experimenting with plant combinations and creating mini-gardens: you can play with the plants, replacing, tweaking and adding when necessary, moving out-sized plants into the garden or to a new home. Working with perennials means that there are times when your window box will look sparse, as the plants become dormant – as would happen in any garden – but without these periods of pause you wouldn't notice the tiny shoots emerging from the soil and have the joy of watching the box come alive each spring.

Pots for balconies and terraces
The size of your garden will dictate, in part, the plants you choose – and remember, if your garden is a roof terrace or balcony there may be weight restrictions to consider. For small rectangular areas like balconies or terraces, I would use the largest containers you can fit and include large statement plants with impressive foliage. It's tempting to choose small plants, but oversized, architectural plants – such as *Fatsia polycarpa* Green Fingers or *Schefflera taiwaniana* – can add structure and texture to a very small space.

Shade gardens / Sacha Leong

I first came across Sacha's idiosyncratic home garden when I delivered some plants. I was totally taken aback when I saw what he had created. Everything was in a mish-mash of containers, there was way more planting than space and hardly any planting repetition — it should have been a mess, but it was completely wonderful. The light ranges from a few hours of afternoon light on the south-facing wall to no light on the north-facing wall. The planting here gets indirect light for most of the day.

'I didn't have an overall plan or much gardening knowledge to begin with, the only goal I had was to have only white flowers in the garden against a dark backdrop (inspired by Sissinghurst Castle Garden in Kent and the Peter Zumthor Serpentine Pavilion in London), and this helped to narrow down the plant choices.'

The view from his kitchen window is a thing of joy. Sacha moves the pots around so whatever is in flower is in view, and his view is always changing. Despite the busyness of the pots, there is a sense of depth and calm from the range and height of foliage.

'The many different plant types I've used means there is constant change throughout the year. It is a simple, timber-decked space that I've packed with pots of multiple sizes and I'm surprised by how much time I can pass in such a tiny garden. There's always some tidying up to do and things to repot. I also find it a meditative place because I can observe all the changes and I'm distracted from the stresses of daily life.'

03

Grow
Discover just the right plants for just the right place

I've compiled a selection of plants that I really like, that work well in varying shade conditions and that suit smaller spaces — it is not meant to be a comprehensive list but should help to get you started. The plants are divided into different categories — bulbs, perennials, ground cover and so on — but many plants fit into a number of categories and there's no right or wrong way to use them.

Autumn through to early winter (before the first frosts) is the best time to plant most herbaceous plants; they will have finished flowering and can use their energy to put down good roots and establish themselves before it gets cold. In an ideal world we would all grow from seed, use plug plants or young plants in 9cm pots: it's more sustainable, cost-effective and makes it easier for plants to establish well in their new environments. But we don't all have access to greenhouses and often a plant in a two-litre pot is all that's available.

Some of the plants listed are harder to find than others but there are plenty of really good specialist nurseries, many of which sell online — I've listed a few of my favourites on page 158.

KEY

◑ Part shade

● Full shade

(DAMP) Damp shade

(DRY) Dry shade

🌱 Suitable for pots or planters

💧 Evergreen

❀ Flowering

Ⓗ Height

Bulbs

Planting bulbs is perhaps the simplest way to garden and is the epitome of forward thinking, faith and hope: small packages pushed into the soil and then left alone, programmed to appear magically in early spring just when we need them most.

Spring bulbs are planted in late autumn and early winter, and they're a lovely way to bring colour into the garden. They work well in woodland-style gardens, but many work in window boxes and planters, too. Known as spring ephemerals (because they flower so early then disappear back into the soil), they can be planted pretty much anywhere in the garden. They are particularly useful under deciduous trees as they flower before the leaves return (the soil underneath evergreens is too dry and the light too limited).

They always look better in large numbers planted in drifts or clumps, so don't hold back when ordering – every spring I look at what's come up and think, 'Lovely, but I should have ordered more.' Most bulbs don't like damp or water-logged soil, so if you have very water-retentive clay soil, add some grit into the planting hole before placing in the bulb, so that they are not sitting in water.

As a general rule of thumb, plant each bulb at a depth that's roughly three times its height and pointy-end up. It needs water in spring, but is happier in dry soil for the rest of the year.

In terms of care, I leave bulbs where they are and add more each autumn to boost the numbers. Some bulbs come back and multiply and some you never see again, so it's a case of watching and learning. With most bulbs, leave the foliage to die back naturally, it's a bit untidy but allows nutrients to pass back to the bulb giving it essential energy for the following spring. Alliums are unusual in that you can cut their foliage off earlier while the plant is still in flower.

Allium siculum / Sicilian honey garlic ↑
◑ ⚱ H: 1M ❄ MAY-JUNE

This is probably my favourite bulb and one of the best alliums for shade. It's a total winner through all its stages of development from its slim paper-wrapped flowerhead, via beautifully coloured chandelier flowers to unusual architectural seedheads. It's also brilliant for pollinators.

A. ursinum / Wild garlic
◑ ● (DRY) ⚱ H: 30CM ❄ APRIL-JUNE

This ancient woodland allium has bright, grass-green leaves and white, star-shaped flowers. They are apt to spread about quickly so keep an eye on them, but a tub full of wild garlic is a lovely thing.

Anemone blanda 'White Splendour' / Winter windflower 'White Splendour' ↑
◑ (DRY) ⚱ H: 20CM ❄ MARCH-APRIL

Anemones are one of the earliest flowering bulbs, delicate in pots and lovely en masse. They have open, white, daisy-like flowers that carpet the ground beneath trees in early spring. I always add these to window boxes.

A. nemorosa / Wood anemone
◑ ● (DRY) H: 20CM ❄ MARCH-APRIL

Similar to *Anemone blanda*, but with smaller flowers and very pretty, deeply divided foliage. Works better naturalised in borders or in grass than in pot. Also try **'Cedric's Pink'** for a pale pink cultivar that darkens with age, and **'Robinsoniana'** for a lovely washed-out pale blue.

Camassia leichtlinii subsp. *suksdorfii* / **Californian quamash**

◑ ⬤ (DRY) (DAMP) H: 1M ✿ MAY-JUNE

These are lovely bulbs and should be grown more often as they are reliable and hardy and will work in tricky spots such as dry or damp shade. They don't like being disturbed, so they're not great for pots. There's no need to lift once planted. **'Alba'** has tall, sturdy stems with star-shaped, creamy-white flowers. Also try **'Pink Star'** for pale pink flowers (though this is harder to get hold of). And **'Blue Melody'**, which is a shorter cultivar that's about 45cm high with pale blue flowers.

Convallaria majalis / **Lily of the valley**

◑ ⬤ ⚱ H: 15CM ✿ MARCH-APRIL

These are one of the few bulbs that don't mind clay soil. They may take a while to establish, but will spread if happy. The tiny, white, bell-shaped flowers are beautifully scented. There's a really pretty pale pink cultivar, **C. majalis var. rosea**, which reaches 25cm.

Cyclamen coum / **Eastern cyclamen**

◑ ⬤ (DRY) ⚱ H: 10CM ✿ JANUARY-MARCH

Delicate clumps of pink and white flowers with small, kidney-shaped foliage often splashed with silver. These will spread around if happy.

C. hederifolium / **Ivy-leaved cyclamen** ↑

◑ ⬤ (DRY) ⚱ H: 10CM

✿ SEPTEMBER-NOVEMBER

Nodding flowers with pink reflexed petals in autumn; for white flowers, opt for **C. hederifolium var. hederifolium f. albiflorum** (pictured). Both are useful under trees. Plant in clumps in late summer for autumn flowers.

Eranthis hyemalis / **Winter aconite**

◑ ⬤ ⚱ H: 10CM ✿ FEBRUARY-MARCH

Sarah Raven describes these as looking like miniature water lilies. Buttercup-yellow with a ruff of green foliage, they are one of the earliest flowerers and as pretty in a window box as they are in drifts under trees. They spread around but don't like being moved.

Fritillaria meleagris /
Snake's head fritillary → ↘
◑ ⚱ H:10CM ❄ APRIL-MAY

There are lots of really interesting
fritillaries and they are perfect for
up-close plantings in pots or planters
as well as for naturalising in beds
or lawns. They do need some light
so choose a position in part shade.
Meleagris is the most commonly seen
species, with its delicate nodding
flowers (which can be pale pink
through to an intense moody purple)
with a distinctive chequerboard
pattern. There's a magical, pure-white
cultivar too. **F. verticillata** has pale
greenish-white flowers and is much
taller, at 60cm. **F. elwesii** (at 30cm) has
unusual striped, dark-purple and olive
colouring – the flowers are like little
humbugs from an old-fashioned sweet
shop. And **F. uva-vulpis**, also 30cm,
is completely charming with purplish-
brown, nodding flowers trimmed with
a golden yellow.

Galanthus nivalis /
Common snowdrop
◑ ● ⟨DRY⟩ ⚱ H:10CM ❄ JANUARY-MARCH

No garden should be without
snowdrops. There are many cultivars
available, though I always come back to
this, our native snowdrop. Plant bulbs
in clumps, though success is more
likely when bought and planted 'in the
green' (as flowering bulbs) in February
or March. There is little better than a
small vase of snowdrops by your bed.

Hyacinthoides non-scripta / English bluebell ↑

◑ ● H: 30CM ❄ APRIL-MAY

The inky-blue, scented, nodding bells of this English bluebell are smaller than the Spanish cultivar and their colour is more intense. Sometimes slow to naturalise, but worth the wait.

Leucojum aestivum / Summer snowflake →

◑ ♈ H: 45CM ❄ APRIL-MAY

I love these oversized snowdrops. They are excellent for instant impact and work as brilliantly in a large pot as they do in a partially shaded bed. They are often listed as needing full sun, but I find them really unfussy about conditions and they grow happily under the trees in my garden.

Muscari / Grape hyacinth

◑ ♈ H: 15CM ❄ MARCH-APRIL

These mainly come in a variety of shades of blue (though there is also a white and a pale pink cultivar) and are perfect for pots. I dot them in among the ferns, where they really sing. They are easy to grow and care for, but are worth lifting and dividing in summer as they spread readily (see page 144). *M. armeniacum* is a deep, deep sky-blue, while *M. latifolium* is a more showy cultivar with a sky-blue top and a darker blue base that's almost purple. My favourite is *M. armeniacum* **'Valerie Finnis'**, which is a pale powder-blue and is the thing I enjoy looking out for the most every spring. All muscari foliage can look a bit messy after flowering, so tuck leaves inside the rim of the pot or window box until they've gone over.

Narcissus / Daffodil

◑ ⚱ ✳ APRIL–MAY

There are so many beautiful narcissi, it's almost impossible to choose. I think they are essential to any garden, especially if you only have a few pots or a window box. **N. bulbocodium Golden Bells Group** is a favourite. Just 15cm tall, these little daffs have bright yellow hooped skirts. I have some dotted around underneath my silver birch and they never fail to make me smile – a handful of these in an old terracotta pot is a lovely present for someone's windowsill. **N. poeticus var. recurvus** is taller, at 45cm, and one I always use. Simple white petals meet a deep orange-yellow corolla; it's a complete classic and smells amazing. **'Actaea'** is similar and comes out a month earlier. **'Tête-à-tête'** also flowers a little earlier, from March, and is just 15cm tall. It's a bright yellow, cheerful mini daff, ideal if you don't have much space – a hardworking little thing. And finally **'Reggae'** reaches 35cm and it has really lovely pinky-peach flowers.

Scilla siberica / Siberian squill ↑

◑ (DRY) ⚱ H:15CM ✳ APRIL–MAY

Expect pretty blue flowers that look dainty but are really hardy and happily self-seed.

Tulipa sylvestris / Wild tulip →

◑ (DRY) ⚱ H:30CM ✳ MARCH–APRIL

Most tulips prefer full sun but this golden yellow, lemon-scented wild tulip works really well in part shade. Once established it will keep coming back. It is less showy than many tulips but one of my favourites. These, like all tulips, prefer to be planted later in the year – November or early December is fine.

Climbers

Although most climbers aren't suited to deep shade, many like their roots shaded as they grow towards the sun and there are some that are definitely suitable for north-facing walls. If you are planting them in the ground, make sure they are around 50cm away from any walls or fences so they are not in a rain shadow and can receive rain. You also need to give them adequate support. Clematis can look beautiful scrambling through trees, but plant it 1m from the trunk and then train it towards the tree. Pots are fine for most climbers if they are a generous size – I'd say at least 45cm tall and wide – but you need to ensure they don't dry out.

← *Akebia quinata* / **Chocolate vine**
● ◐ ⛏ H: 6M ✳ APRIL-MAY
A very vigorous and very pretty twining vine with clusters of deep burgundy, scented flowers. I've grown this on north-facing walls and in pots. It's reliable, but doesn't like its roots being disturbed. This can be semi-evergreen in sheltered spots. Requires very little pruning. *A. longeracemosa* is similar, but drips with racemes of wisteria-like flowers.

Cissus striata / Ivy of Uruguay ↓
◐ ◊ H: 10M ✳ JUNE-JULY
Slender but vigorous evergreen climber with delicate ivy-shaped leaves from the same family (*Vitaceae*) as the Virginia creeper (*Parthenocissus*), but it's not invasive. Light-green flowers arrive in summer that pollinators love, followed by berries. A more delicate alternative to ivy if you can find it.

Clematis 'Apple Blossom'

◐ 🌱 🍃 H: 6M ❄ MARCH–APRIL

Expect a pinkish tinge on the flowers of this popular evergreen clematis. Strongly scented, it's very vigorous but prefers a sheltered position as the leaves can brown in windy situations.

C. cirrhosa var. purpurascens 'Freckles'

◐ 🌱 🍃 H: 6M ❄ DECEMBER–APRIL

Long-flowering, creamy white blooms with purple freckles. Useful flowerer in winter months which then goes dormant through the summer. A clematis that likes a sheltered spot.

C. 'Elizabeth'

◐ H: 8M ❄ MAY–JUNE

A very vigorous, highly scented, montana clematis. Open, pale pink flowers can cover a wall in no time.

C. rehderiana / Nodding virgin's bower

◐ H: 8M ❄ JULY–OCTOBER

An unusual and very vigorous clematis with small, velvety, pale-yellow, scented flowers and a terrible name. Needs space and would suit a woodland planting style. It's worth seeking out as it smells lovely. Cut back early winter to keep it in check.

C. viorna / Blue virgin's bower

◐ 🌱 H: 3M ❄ JUNE–SEPTEMBER

A deep violet-blue, very dainty bell-shaped flower. An unusual species; I got mine from Great Dixter's nursery.

C. 'White Columbine'

◐ 🌱 H: 3M ❄ APRIL–MAY

Most early-flowering clematis prefer partially shaded spots. Naturally found up mountains, alpinas such as 'White Columbine' are very robust and don't really need much attention – they are my favourite of the three groups of clematis. The bell-like flowers are delicate, the foliage is pretty and they usually have great seedheads. This is a lovely white cultivar. I also like **'Frances Rivis'**, which is similar, but with a violet-blue, slightly twisted flower.

Hedera helix 'Green Ripple' / Common ivy 'Green Ripple'

◐ ● 🌱 🍃 H: 4M

An ivy cultivar with fresh green foliage. It's vigorous and great for providing a green backdrop to other plants. Ivy has a poor reputation, but it is actually a really useful plant for wildlife, especially through winter when there's not much else around.

Holboellia coriacea / Sausage vine →

◐ ● 🌱 🍃 H: 4M ❄ APRIL–MAY

A really vigorous evergreen climber with lots of fresh green foliage in spring. It can tolerate full shade, but needs sun to flower. Lovely fragrance on pale mauve flowers.

Humulus lupulus 'Aureus' / Golden hop

◐ ☕ H: 6M ❄ JULY-AUGUST

Although often seen in full sun, this can tolerate partial shade. In bright light it is vigorous and puts out runners, but I have one in a pot in my shady lightwell and it grows slowly towards the light. It has a beautiful leaf shape and is great for lighting up dark walls. The hop flowers dry beautifully.

Hydrangea petiolaris / Climbing hydrangea

◐ ● ☕ H: 6M ❄ JUNE-JULY

This climber is initially slow to get going, but once it's established it goes fast! Great for covering a north-facing wall, it can be lightly cut back after flowering if you don't want it to become too bushy. The large, elegant, lace-cap flowers also look great into winter as seedheads.

Lonicera caprifolium / Italian woodbine

◐ ☕ H: 6M ❄ MAY-AUGUST

Honeysuckles prefer part shade and fertile soil. This one has beautiful peach-pink flowers. **L. henryi** is evergreen and reaches 8m – a more vigorous climber, it has larger foliage than many honeysuckles. It's not as pretty as some, but provides a useful evergreen backdrop to other plants. **L. periclymenum 'Graham Thomas'** is smaller at 6m and can flower into September with soft yellow flowers. It's fast growing and highly scented.

Muehlenbeckia complexa / Maidenhair vine ↑

◐ ☕ ◊ H: 3M

Tiny little leaves on wiry stems make this an elegant choice. I use it in lots of pots and planters as it looks so good tumbling over the edge. It's a great climber, too. Be warned, it is a fast-grower and can take over – if it gets too big you can always dig it out and divide it (see page 144).

Parthenocissus henryana / Chinese virginia creeper

◐ ● ☕ H: 6M

This is super-vigorous and another good option for north-facing walls. It's great at covering large areas quickly, and the silvery markings on this species' bronzy-green foliage (and the later autumnal colour) are really gorgeous.

Schizophragma hydrangeoides / Japanese hydrangea vine →

◑ ✄ H: 6M ❊ JULY

This climber is great for a small space and its large, creamy, lace-cap flowers are often tinged with pink. The cultivar pictured is *S. h.* var. *concolor* **'Moonlight'** and lights up this dark corner beautifully.

Trachelospermum jasminoides / Star jasmine ↘

◑ ✄ ◊ H: 9M ❊ JUNE-AUGUST

Highly scented white flowers and very vigorous growth make this a popular option. It is said to prefer full sun, but I find it works well in shade too, it just doesn't flower as generously. It does like a sheltered spot. As an alternative, **T. asiaticum 'Pink Showers'** is a lovely pink-flowering cultivar.

Roses

All these roses have good fragrance – it seems silly to me to have a rose that doesn't have scent, no matter how pretty the flowers. They are also all repeat flowerers, which means they can flower any time (on and off) between late spring and early winter in the UK. Roses are greedy plants, so they do require mulching and feeding in spring to really perform well. If possible, buy and plant bare-root roses in winter. It's cheaper than buying them in pots and they establish better.

Lady of Shalott
H: 1.3M (SHRUB)

This has a lovely airy structure and scented, sunset-coloured flowers. What more could you ask for?

Mme Alfred Carrière
H: 7.5M (CLIMBER)

Famously used in Sissinghurst's White Garden, this rose is not always fast to flower, but once established you can't really beat the blooms or their fragrance. It is very tall, so prefers a high wall, arch or tree to climb up.

Munstead Wood
H: 1M (SHRUB)

With deep crimson flowers, this rose works surprisingly well with ferns and grasses, its dark, sultry colouring cutting through the green. Full sunlight is always recommended, but it will do fine in part shade if it's getting 4–6 hours of light.

The Generous Gardener
H: 4.5M (CLIMBER)

Fast-growing with the palest of pink flowers that are very graceful. It's in the darkest corner of my garden, unceremoniously planted behind a shed, and it has loads of fragrant flowers every summer.

The Lady of the Lake
H: 3-4M (RAMBLER)

Small, semi-double cups of pale pink flowers with a citrus scent. This keeps going from late May through much of summer in my garden, with a second flush that often takes it to October.

The Lark Ascending
H: 1.5M (SHRUB)

Extremely pretty, loose, open, apricot-coloured flowers. It does need a bit of space as it can grow up to 1.5m wide as well as tall, but it has a long flowering season from May through to late autumn.

Top left Mme Alfred Carrière **Top right** The Lady of the Lake **Bottom left** The Generous Gardener **Bottom right** The Lark Ascending

Shrubs

These shrubs are small enough and tolerant enough to survive in part shade. They are broadly familiar with being part of the understorey and therefore making the most of the light that filters down through the trees above them. This is a limited list as I've focused on plants for smaller spaces. It's worth noting that if they are planted in pots, shrubs won't reach the maximum height specified here, which isn't always a bad thing.

Aralia elata / **Angelica tree**
  (DAMP) H: 2M JULY-AUGUST

This architectural shrub forms impressive clumps with arching stems and large, bright green foliage that is good for drawing the eye. Greenish-white flowers in summer are followed by purplish-black berries in autumn.

Chaenomeles speciosa / **Quince** ↓
  H: 1.5M  MARCH-MAY

Although quinces tend to look best trained along a wall where the flowers really shine, I have this shrub growing against the railing that overhangs the pavement and it cheers me up every time I see it in flower. It's a definite harbinger of spring. Alternatively, **'Geisha Girl'** has pretty peach flowers and is a more compact cultivar than a lot of quinces – ideal by a sheltered wall, though I've also seen one that looks stunning planted in a large stone pot. Both are fairly slow-growing.

Danae racemosa / **Poet's laurel** ↑
   H: 1M

A slow-growing evergreen for some graceful texture. Its bright, shiny foliage can completely lift a shady border or balcony and it has a really elegant form. Autumn berries are loved by the birds.

Euphorbia mellifera / **Honey spurge**
 H: 1.8M ❀ MAY–JUNE

Bushy in full sun, this semi-evergreen shrub tends to be airier in shadier spots. Likes a bit of shelter, so it is happy in cities and also works in a large pot as a statement plant. Amazing honey-scented flowers arrive in early summer.

× *Fatshedera lizei* / **Fat-headed lizzy**
  H: 2M

An unusual but very interesting cross between an ivy and fatsia, this plant works as a climber or a shrub. It needs tying in as a climber and regular pruning as a shrub, but both look great in the right situation. Prefers a sheltered spot.

Fatsia japonica / **Castor oil plant** ↓
   H: 4M

A classic shade plant. If you want something evergreen, low-maintenance and fast-growing, this is the one. It does prefer a bit of shelter, but is perfect for bringing some tropical vibes to a dark corner. Keep in a pot if you don't want it to get too big.

Fatsia polycarpa Green Fingers / Many-fruited aralia Green Fingers ↑

◑ ✄ ◊ H: 3M

A newish cultivar of *F. polycarpa*, with lighter and airier foliage that works well in lots of planting schemes. Good in a pot, too. I'm always raving about this plant as it is very useful; one of my favourites for structure and impact in a small space.

Fuchsia 'Hawkshead'

◑ ✄ H: 1M ❋ JUNE-OCTOBER

I know what you're thinking: fuchsias are frumpy and garish, but I promise this one has elegant, elongated, white flowers that drip prettily from the foliage for several months over summer. Lovely paired with large ferns and works well in a pot.

F. magellanica var. molinae / Maiden's blush fuchsia

◑ ✄ H: 1.5M ❋ JUNE-OCTOBER

Yes, another fuchsia! This one is a delicate wonder with long-flowering, pale blooms that sing against its foliage. It's great in a shady area and comes into its own in late summer. It can be trained against a wall or grown in a pot. It's also good for pollinators.

Hebe 'Green Globe' / Shrubby Veronica 'Green Globe'

◑ ✄ ◊ H: 40M ❋ JUNE-AUGUST

A useful dwarf shrub with a naturally domed shape that's useful as edging or to provide structure between frothy or ferny planting. Tiny, white, nectar-rich flowers emerge in summer. It needs very little attention, and the same can be said of **H. ochracea 'James Stirling'**, which grows up to 60cm tall and flowers a little earlier. It has much lighter yellow-green foliage, similar to that of a conifer, and again the rounded mound shape is useful for structure – it's a bit more pillowy but very tactile.

Hydrangea paniculata 'Limelight' →

◑ ✄ H: 2.5M ❋ JUNE-OCTOBER

This is my favourite hydrangea. It has pale lime-green flowers that fade to a soft white and then dirty-pink as they age. Beautiful in winter when the flowers have dried on long stems, it is also great for wildlife. It just about works in a pot – I've had one for three years in a large pot and it's still happy.

Hydrangea quercifolia /
Oak-leaved hydrangea

◐ ⚊ H: 1.5M ❋ JULY–SEPTEMBER

Really handsome hydrangea with large, dark green foliage that moves through shades of orange and dark red in autumn. The panicles of creamy-white flowers turn pinkish-brown and the seedheads hold through winter. This hardworking plant is great in a large pot or planter on a wide balcony.

Mahonia eurybracteata 'Soft Caress' / Oregon grape 'Soft Caress'

● ◐ ⚊ ◊ H: 1M ❋ AUGUST–OCTOBER

I'm not a huge mahonia fan, but to me this one is the most attractive. It's evergreen, elegant and *not* prickly; it also has a pleasing mounding form. I don't love the yellow flowers, but I do love the foliage and grow it just for that. It's easy to look after and not particularly vigorous. Ideal in an evergreen courtyard garden and would work in a large pot.

Pittosporum tenuifolium
'Golf Ball' ↗

● ◐ ⚊ ◊ H: 1.2M ❋ MAY–JUNE

This is a useful, rounded, evergreen shrub that, like hebe, provides structure among frothy planting and only requires an annual prune. It prefers a sheltered spot and just about takes full shade. The flowers are small, but good for pollinators and they smell delicious.

P. tobira 'Nanum'

◐ ⚊ ◊ H: 75CM ❋ APRIL–JUNE

A smaller cultivar than *P. tenuifolium*, with larger, darker and more shiny foliage and honey-scented flowers. It similarly provides useful structure and evergreen interest.

Rhus thibetanus / Ghost bramble

◐ H: 2M

I love this for the name alone. This arching shrub can get prickly and dense, so not ideal for a small balcony where you might brush past it, but if you have the room it provides the most beautiful white skeleton structure in winter.

Sambucus nigra f. *porphyrophylla* 'Eva' / Elder 'Eva' →

◑ ⛆ H: 2.5M ❄ MAY-JUNE

Can become large and needs some sun, but is great if you're after dark filigree foliage. It has pale pink flowerheads. Works in a large pot, where it remains a more manageable size.

Sarcococca confusa / Sweet box

● ◑ ⛆ ◊ H: 2M ❄ DECEMBER-MARCH

Mounds of evergreen foliage and deeply sweet-scented, white flowers in winter make it a treat. It is slow-growing, works in a pot and I recommend placing it somewhere you can smell the flowers. **Winter Gem** is more compact at 50cm, with grey-olive foliage. Same lovely fragrance.

Sorbaria sorbifolia 'Sem'

◑ ⛆ H: 1.2M ❄ JULY-AUGUST

A soft-mounded shrub with ferny foliage and white flowers. Fresh foliage emerges in pinky tones, moving to green before turning red in autumn. Sorbarias can become large, but 'Sem' is compact. You can just about get away with planting it in a big pot.

Viburnum × *burkwoodii* / Burkwood viburnum →

◑ ⛆ H: 2.5M ❄ APRIL-MAY

I grow this in a container, but it's a very large container. It has white flower clusters, that smell amazing, plus it has an airy shape. **'Anne Russell'** is slightly smaller, but both are tolerant of exposed sites and pollution.

Planting combinations / For pots and borders

←
Brunnera macrophylla
'Jack Frost',
Anemone blanda
You can't go wrong
with this early-spring
combination; it's simple,
but very effective and
makes me happy every
year! These plants are
growing under a birch
tree to give a woodland
feel to a shady corner.

→
Asplenium scolopendrium,
Adiantum venustum,
Polypodium vulgare
A low-maintenance
combination of three
ferns make a lovely
evergreen planter. If you
have very limited space
and light, this on its own
will work a treat. There
are also some snowdrops
buried in there, which will
make their way through.

←
Briza maxima, Astilbe
'Federsee' (× arendsii)
Greater quaking grass
nearly always comes with
a label that says 'full sun',
but I find it grows well
with far less light. The
astilbe was left over from
a job, and I planted it in a
tiny space at the back of
my garden where it pops
up in summer for a few
weeks; I really love the
colour it brings.

Ground cover

Ground-cover plants spread like a carpet, low to the ground across the soil. They can hold your planting choices together, weaving in and out of taller species, protecting the soil from erosion and helping to suppress weeds. A municipal approach, particularly in tough areas like dense shade, would be to use a single vigorous plant such as a periwinkle (*Vinca*) or pachysandra, but this restricts biodiversity. If you can, use a patchwork of low-growing plants – it will look nicer and is better for the environment. Some of the plants in this section have a pot symbol alongside them as they can also work in a large planter.

Alchemilla alpina /
Alpine lady's mantle
◑ H: 20CM ❄ JUNE-SEPTEMBER

A diminutive version of *Alchemilla mollis* (see Perennials on page 110) with beautiful, silver-edged, palm-shaped, serrated foliage, chartreuse flowers and a tendency to spread into cracks, though not nearly as vigorously as *A. mollis*.

Opposite A patchwork of low-growing plants in a north-facing bed including sweet woodruff (*Galium odoratum*), water avens (*Geum rivale*), epimediums and a hardy geranium

Anemone sylvestris /
Snowdrop windflower
◑ H: 40M ❄ APRIL-JUNE

A pretty white windflower with drooping flowerheads that turn into fluffy seedheads. It's not keen on clay soil, but if it's happy it'll form sweet-smelling clumps.

Asarum europaeum / Wild ginger ↓
● ◑ 💧 H:15CM

Shiny, heart-shaped leaves form a beautiful and effective creeping ground cover, but wild ginger is slow growing so you will need patience. It is semi-evergreen but can be evergreen in sheltered spots once established.

93

Cardamine trifolia /
Three-leaved cuckoo flower
● ◐ (DRY) 🌱 💧 H: 30CM ❄ MARCH-APRIL

Neat, trifoliate leaves with tiny, pretty white flowers on dainty stems in early spring. Drought-tolerant once established. Works in pots and is good for pollinators. Like so many plants, I wish it was more readily available.

Cymbalaria muralis /
Ivy-leaved toadflax ↓
◐ (DRY) 🌱 🌿 H: 10CM ❄ APRIL-SEPTEMBER

A diminutive, mat-forming plant with delicate foliage and tiny, pale mauve, snap-dragon-shaped flowers. It is often found in walls and cracks in the pavement softening hard edges. You can propagate it easily by pulling off a little piece of rooted stem and planting it elsewhere.

Brunnera macrophylla /
Siberian bugloss ↑
● ◐ (DAMP) (DRY) H: 40CM ❄ APRIL-MAY

An invaluable, spreading perennial with green, heart-shaped leaves and sprays of intense forget-me-not-blue flowers in spring. Essentially, this is a better behaved forget-me-not (*Myosotis*). It does like a bit of moisture, but once established will tolerate dry shade and is great underneath deciduous trees. For white flowers, go for **'Alba'**, and for larger foliage with beautiful silver veins, plant **'Jack Frost'** (pictured). I use this one the most, as it's so good at lighting up dark spots.

Epimedium / **Barrenwort** →

● ◐ (DRY) ❦ ◊ ❄ MARCH-APRIL

Epimediums are delicate-looking plants that are actually very hardy and great in dry shade underneath trees. There are an increasing amount of available cultivars and it's easy to be captivated by their delicacy – I find it hard to pass a new one by. My favourites include the reliably tough **E. × *versicolor* 'Sulphureum'** (pictured), which reaches about 35cm and has sulphur-yellow flowers that are often partially hidden by foliage that's a coppery red in early spring. And also **E × *warleyense* 'Orangekönigin'**, which is taller, at 50cm, and has heart-shaped leaves and intricate peachy-orange flowers floating on wiry stems. **E × *youngianum* 'Niveum'** reaches 30cm, and while it's not evergreen it is irresistibly delicate with the most beautiful pure white, floating flowers.

Fragaria vesca / **Wild strawberry** →

◐ (DRY) ❦ H: 30CM ❄ APRIL-JUNE

This thrives in part shade and spreads via runners. The fruits are tiny and sweet. There's a variegated cultivar called **'Patchwork'** which really sings.

Galium odoratum / **Sweet woodruff**

● ◐ H: 35CM ❄ MAY-JUNE

This is one of my favourite ground-cover plants (pictured on page 92). Scented green foliage with white starry flowers through spring, it is fast spreading and entirely edible. It's also semi-evergreen in sheltered locations.

G. nodosum 'Silverwood'

◑ (DRY) ⚰ H: 30CM ✳ MAY-SEPTEMBER

A woodland classic, this long-flowering geranium self-seeds and spreads around. It has soft white flowers on bright green foliage.

← *G. robertianum* 'Album' / Herb Robert 'Album'

◑ ⚰ H: 20CM ✳ MAY-SEPTEMBER

A lovely white version of the usual pinky-purple herb Robert that self-seeds so freely. It's less promiscuous, but once you have 'Album' it will happily spread around.

G. sanguineum 'Album' / Bloody cranesbill 'Album'

◑ (DRY) ⚰ H: 35CM ✳ MAY-JUNE

Lots of bright white, partially reflexed flowers on dark green foliage. One of the prettiest geraniums out there.

Lamium / Deadnettle →

◑ (DRY) ⚰ H: 20CM ✳ JUNE-AUGUST

All deadnettles are excellent at supporting pollinators, especially bees. **L. galeobdolon** is a vigorous spreader, so perhaps not suitable for small gardens, but I do love it for its hooded yellow flowers. **L. maculatum 'Pink Pewter'** is also a favourite, with silvery, spreading foliage, sometimes splashed with pink spots, and with sugar-pink flowers that light up a dark corner or a pot. **'White Nancy'** (pictured opposite) is the same, but with white flowers. Both are absolute bee magnets. For another deadnettle, see page 119.

Geranium / Cranesbill

So many geraniums work as ground-cover plants in both sun and shade, with a number useful for dry shade. They definitely benefit from being cut back hard after their first flowers: you'll get fresh green foliage and hopefully a second flush of flowers. Most are spreading, so you can dig up clumps, divide them and give to friends if you have too much (see page 144). They are also fantastic for pollinators.

G. macrorrhizum 'White-Ness'

● ◑ (DRY) ⚰ H: 40CM ✳ MAY-JUNE

This geranium is excellent for dry shade, with bright green, evergreen foliage and very dainty and pretty white flowers.

Ophiopogon planiscapus / Mondo grass

◐ (DRY) ⚘ ☗ H: 15CM

An evergreen, grass-like and grass-green perennial, tolerant of dry shade. Can be effective at adding movement and texture to a border and looks good lining a path. **'Kokuryu'** is not good in dry shade, but its almost-black, fine, strappy leaves have undeniable impact, especially when planted with drifts of snowdrops or with bright green fern foliage. Pale mauve summer flower spikes are followed by berries.

Oxalis acetosella / Wood sorrel

● ◐ (DRY) H: 10CM ❁ APRIL-MAY

Delicate, clover-shaped foliage with small, mauve-white flowers in late spring and early summer. A really lovely, spreading woodland plant. Grows under trees, but doesn't like competition.

Persicaria affinis 'Donald Lowndes' / Knotweed 'Donald Lowndes' ↑

◐ (DAMP) H: 45CM ❁ JULY-AUGUST

Semi-evergreen, 'Donald Lowndes' is a low-growing persicaria with neat foliage and pinkish-red, upright flower spires. *P. runcinata* **'Purple Fantasy'** (pictured) is taller, at 60cm, and has brilliantly showy foliage that's arrow shaped and a pale minty-green with a purple and silver chevron; it flowers July–September. It's also good in a pot or in a shady corner, and is seen here with *P. microcephala* **'Red Dragon'** – both are vigorous spreaders.

Saxifraga × umbrosa / London pride

● ◐ ✿ ◊ H: 45CM ✽ FEBRUARY-MAY

This old-fashioned plant has small rosettes of evergreen, mat-forming foliage (great for suppressing weeds) and frothy bursts of tiny, star-like, pale pink flowers on wiry stems in spring. Great in pots or planters as well as ground cover or at the front of borders. **S. × geum** flowers a little later in May and June and reaches just 20cm tall. Its neat, evergreen foliage and little sprays of white-pink flowers are gorgeous popping through ferns, grasses and hostas at the front of a planter.

Symphytum / Comfrey

● ◐ (DRY) H: 50CM ✽ MAY-JUNE

You do need a bit of space to grow comfrey – it has large leaves and deep roots that aren't always easy to remove – but it makes excellent ground cover. If you have a bit of garden that you're happy to let go a little, a clump of **'Hidcote Blue'** or **'Hidcote Pink'** will bring all the bees to the yard. You can cut it down after flowering to make comfrey tea, which is a brilliant fertiliser (see page 141). The gentle gradation of colour on the flowers is beautiful, but can get a bit lost in the foliage so I often put a few of them in a vase so I can see them properly.

Top left Symphytum 'Hidcote Pink' **Top right** Viola cornuta 'Alba' **Bottom left** V. hederacea **Bottom right** V. odorata

Vinca minor f. alba 'Gertrude Jekyll' / Small white periwinkle 'Gertrude Jekyll'

● ◐ (DRY) ◊ H: 20CM ✽ APRIL-SEPTEMBER

An evergreen spreader with bright white flowers and a long-flowering season. More compact and not as vigorous as other vincas, but still fast growing. It can be broken up with deadnettles or violas. Useful in really tricky shade.

Viola cornuta 'Alba' / Horned violet 'Alba'

● ◐ ✿ H: 15CM ✽ APRIL-AUGUST

Fresh, chalk-white flowers on bright semi-evergreen foliage; if cut back, it will keep a neater form and flower again in autumn.

V. hederacea / Australian violet

◐ ✿ H: 15CM ✽ APRIL-OCTOBER

A spreading violet with white and purple flowers. As with the other violets, deadhead to prolong flowering.

V. odorata / Sweet violet

◐ ✿ H: 20CM ✽ FEBRUARY-MARCH

This mat-forming viola has deep blue-purple, sweet-smelling, edible flowers and heart-shaped foliage. Makes an interesting alternative to a lawn.

V. sororia 'Freckles' / Violet 'Freckles'

◐ ✿ H: 20CM ✽ APRIL-JULY

Another spreading violet with dark green leaves and the loveliest white-pale blue flowers freckled with blue-violet spots.

Ferns

Ferns are one of the first plants people think of for shade. Evergreen options can add structure and winter interest, and the perennials often have the most magical unfurling foliage in fresh greens, coppery-pinks or silvers – there is a wonderful variety of foliage shape and size to explore. Some ferns take to dry shade, while some really need to be kept moist – if you don't let these dry out and mulch them regularly they'll work hard. Pretty much all ferns grow well in pots as they have shallow roots. A combination of three ferns with contrasting foliage in a large pot is a winner for a shady corner (see page 90). There are so many more I could include in this list, but these are the ones I return to time and again.

***Adiantum venustum* /**
Evergreen maidenhair ↑
● ◗ ✿ 🍃 H: 20CM

This fern's soft, delicate foliage needs protection from the sun but the plant is hardy. If the elegant fronds crisp up, cut them back, water the plant and have patience. I have this in a planter and rarely give it attention, but it thrives. *A. pedatum* (pictured) is slightly more structural, with finger-like fronds on black wiry stems. Cut dried stems back to encourage new growth.

← ***Asplenium scolopendrium* /**
Hart's tongue fern
● ◗ (DAMP) (DRY) ✿ H: 40CM

A UK native, evergreen fern with upright, strappy, structural leaves.

Its bright, leathery fronds provide useful contrast and are really hardy. Will tolerate dry shade once established.

Athyrium filix-femina / Lady fern
  (DRY) H: 1M

This spreading deciduous fern has bright, fresh green fronds in spring. I use this a lot as I love the colour. It can tolerate dry shade once established. Cut back the old fronds in winter.

A. niponicum var. pictum / Japanese painted fern
H: 30CM

A soft, green and silver-grey deciduous fern with a red-flushed central spine and elegant shape that's striking in planters. Provides a beautiful contrast to other ferns.

← Blechnum spicant / Deer fern
  (DAMP) H: 60CM

A small and neat tufted evergreen that's native to the UK. If you're planting several ferns, this is a good contrast to the more lacy, floppy types. Prefers damp soil, but fine in a pot that's watered regularly.

Cystopteris fragilis / Brittle bladder fern
  (DAMP) H: 30CM

Lacy, deciduous, grey-green fronds make this a very attractive fern. It's quite hard to find, unfortunately, and too small for a border, but perfect in a stone pot placed right where you can see it.

Dicksonia antarctica / Soft tree fern ↗
 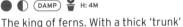 (DAMP) H: 4M

The king of ferns. With a thick 'trunk' (which is actually matted fibrous roots) and huge fronds, this tree fern provides height, drama and lushness. It can tolerate full shade and prefers moisture-retentive soil and a sheltered spot as it needs protection against frosts and from the sun – this makes it perfect for a small courtyard garden if you have room for its fronds, which can reach up 2m in length. It will be okay in a large pot, but prefers being in the ground. Tree ferns have a reputation for being high maintenance, but in the right position they are actually pretty easy to look after. They don't like drying out, so water both the crown (the top part, where the fronds emerge) and the fibrous 'trunk' really well on first planting and throughout every summer. They are very slow-growing (about 5cm a year), but feeding during the growing season can give them a boost. If it looks as if it's going to be very cold, carefully add a clump of straw to the crown of the plant to protect it. You can tie the fronds together for further protection. Don't cut off any brown, dried fronds until they are completely droopy; when you do cut them, leave at least 15cm of the stem as this will eventually become part of the new trunk-like growth.

Dryopteris erythrosora / Japanese shield fern →

  (DAMP) (DRY) ☙ H: 75CM

A deciduous, compact fern with beautiful, copper-pink fronds that make a striking contrast to all the green foliage. I use this in my window boxes. It can take more light than a lot of ferns and will tolerate dry shade once established.

Matteuccia struthiopteris / Shuttlecock fern

 ● ◑ (DAMP) ⚱ H: 1.5M

Beautiful, large, upright fern with vivid green foliage that gracefully unfurls into feathery fronds. Spreads by stolons (horizontal runners) so it's very easy to propagate (see page 144). It's said to like damp conditions, though I've seen it grow happily in dry soil.

Osmunda regalis / Royal fern

 ● ◑ (DAMP) ⚱ H: 2.5M

This fern's toothed fronds can reach over 1m tall and form large, unusual rusty-brown 'flowers' in autumn that work well with other fern foliage. It can grow in most conditions but does prefer it moist; it can take full shade as well as a fair amount of sun.

Polypodium vulgare / Common polypody

 ◑ (DRY) ⚱ H: 60CM

Another UK native evergreen fern, not dissimilar, but bigger than *Blechnum spicant* (see page 102). It can tolerate a fair amount of sun and is good in dry shade once established. I use this a lot in planters as it is a moderate size and adds evergreen structure.

Polystichum polyblepharum / Japanese lace fern

 ● ◑ (DAMP) ⚱ H: 75CM

Elegant and evergreen with dark green mature fronds; new fronds are covered in golden hair and flip backwards as they unfurl, temporarily resembling tassels. This one prefers damp shade but has been known to grow happily in drier conditions.

P. setiferum / Soft shield fern

 ● ◑ (DRY) ⚱ H: 1.5M

A hardy, large and spreading evergreen fern that's fairly drought-tolerant once established. It looks amazing at full size in a large pot. If you're brave and cut it right back in March, it will be thriving again by April. *P. tussimense* (Korean rock fern) reaches 45cm and isn't right for dry shade, but is a lovely little evergreen fern with glossy green leaves with contrasting black scales.

Top left *Osmunda regalis* **Top right** *Polystichum polyblepharum* **Bottom left** *P. setiferum* **Bottom right** *P. tussimense*

Planting combinations / For pots and borders

→
***Tellima grandiflora,
Brunnera, Luzula nivea,
Meconopsis***
This foursome is probably
my favourite bit of my
garden at any time of
year. There is something
calming about the pale
greens and forget-me-not
blues and I like the orange
pops of colour that the
poppies give. The tellima
flowers eventually turn
a lovely pinkish-brown.
There is always a lot of
pollinator action around
here, too.

←
***Fatsia japonica, Osmunda
regalis, Ophiopogon
planiscapus, Camellia***
The gloss on the evergreen
fatsia and the flowers of the
camellia work really well
in this very dark spot; the
ophiopogon peeking out at
the bottom adds another
layer of colour and texture.

→
***Arum italicum,
Epimedium* × *warleyense*
'Orangekönigin'**
A good group for dry
shade, though you
can achieve a similar
patchwork of foliage with
any number of shady
ground-cover plants. It's
a great way of adding
interest. The markings and
structure of the arum are
particularly effective here.

Grasses

I love grasses in a shady border. They can really lift the planting by adding movement and a more naturalistic vibe, breaking up clumps of ferns or evergreen shrubs. Many of these work in pots or planters and are invaluable for balcony planting. Most grasses can deal with some shade, but do check the requirements of any not listed here, just in case.

Anemanthele lessoniana / Pheasant's tail grass ↑
● ◑ (DRY) ◒ H: 90CM

An absolute stalwart in my planting, with loose arching mounds and purple-pink flowerheads in summer. Depending on how much sun it gets, it

will turn orange-red over winter. It has the power to pull together planting across a garden, as it works well in both sun and shade. It's short-lived but self-seeds.

Carex divulsa / Grey sedge
● ◑ (DAMP) (DRY) ☗ ◒ H: 75CM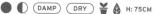

A really useful mound-forming evergreen grass with interesting texture. Works beautifully with ferns and larger grasses and is ideal for the front of borders or in a pot. Dry or damp, sun or shade, it's happy.

Chasmanthium latifolium / Northern sea oats
◑ H: 90CM

This attractive grass has interesting flowers and seedpods that look like flattened ears of oats and it is beautiful dried. It definitely prefers part shade as it needs some light, as well as space to spread. There's a smaller cultivar called **'Little Tickler'**. As with most of these, cut back in spring.

Hakonechloa macra / Japanese forest grass →
● (DAMP) ☗ H: 50CM

A bright green deciduous grass with sprays of flowers in spring. Slow to establish, but so good when it does. It has the most beautiful movement in the wind. Good in pots, at the front of borders and paired with ferns.

Luzula nivea / Snowy wood-rush →
  H: 60CM

Probably my favourite grass for shade as it gives an almost meadowy vibe. Nice and airy with pretty white flowers in spring. Can tolerate dry or damp shade and is evergreen. Cut back dead and old foliage in early spring. **L. sylvatica** is a bit taller with narrower, brighter and greener leaves. I like the understated brown flowerheads that float on arching stems, especially mixed among ferns in a planter. Prefers a bit of moisture, so don't plant in dry shade.

Melica uniflora f. albida / Siberian melic
 H: 60CM

A magical, summery, dainty grass with little seedheads that look like floating grains of rice. It spreads once

established. Use to provide movement in pots or at the front of a border.

Milium effusum 'Aureum' / Bowles's golden grass
 (DAMP) H: 60CM

Compact, yellow-green grass with nodding yellow flowers. This one may divide opinion, but it's hardy and useful in lifting a dark corner or breaking up a lot of dense green.

Sesleria autumnalis / Moor-grass
 H: 90CM

A semi-evergreen, light-coloured, compact, clump-forming grass that's good for all seasons. It has long-lasting, soft grey-silver flower spikes through summer. **S. 'Greenlee Hybrid'** is shorter at 50cm with tiny white flowers on tall spikes. Both prefer part shade and both are useful for holding planting together.

Perennials

There are so many perennials to choose from! I've included as many as there is space for, so try to see this list as a jumping-off point – if you like the look of something, do a little research and see if there are other cultivars with colours or heights you prefer. Finding the right plants that work for you takes time. Since most annuals prefer a sunny spot, perennial plants are essential to the shade gardener. These are wonderful plants that generously return year after year, often bigger and better.

Acanthus mollis / Bear's breeches →
◑ (DRY) ❦ H: 1.5M ✿ JULY-AUGUST

Really impressive, semi-evergreen, glossy foliage meets stately spires of purple and white hooded flowers. It gives instant impact. Once established, it does spread, so be careful if planting in a small space, however a really large planter in a tight spot can look striking. **'Rue Ledan'** is slightly smaller, with silvery foliage and white flowers.

Actaea / Baneberry
◑ (DAMP)

These are very tall, high-impact, late-summer-flowering perennials often with good seedheads for structural interest. A baneberry prefers humus-rich woodland soil, so avoid

if you have dry shade. And do note that the berries are poisonous. **A. matsumurae 'White Pearl'** reaches over 1m and flowers in September and October – slender, scented, white flowerheads become bright green seedheads in winter. **A. simplex 'Prichard's Giant'** is taller (2m) and flowers in June and July. A proper statement plant with lush green foliage and airy, white flowers.

Alchemilla mollis / Lady's mantle ↓
◑ ❦ H: 60CM ✿ MAY-AUGUST

With acid-green flowers and velvety-green foliage, this plant holds drops of rainwater like jewels. Cut it back in early summer to prompt a second flush of flowers.

Anemone × hybrida 'Honorine Jobert' / Japanese anemone 'Honorine Jobert' →

● ◐ (DRY) ⚱ H: 1.2M ❋ JULY–SEPTEMBER

A stalwart when it comes to shade planting, the simple, bright white flowers of the Japanese anemone are elegant and work with many combinations. The plant spreads via runners and it can take over a bit if it's happy, but it's not a bad problem to have. It's fine in dry shade once established and very low maintenance. **'Königin Charlotte'** is a similar size but with pale pink, semi-double flowers.

Aquilegia vulgaris 'Nivea' / Granny's bonnet 'Nivea' →

◐ ⚱ H: 75CM ❋ MAY–JULY

A classic cottage garden flower with distinctive white blooms and delicate foliage. Looks great in a pot against a wall. **'Black Barlow'** has gorgeous, dark purplish pom-pom-shaped flowers – it needs a light background to really set them off.

Arum italicum subsp. *italicum* 'Marmoratum' / Italian arum 'Marmoratum'

◐ (DRY) ⚱ H: 30CM

Expect very distinctive, creamy-green marbled foliage (that's useful for contrast) to appear in spring and hang around for most of the year (pictured on page 107). I was converted when I saw it work beautifully with epimediums in a tough patch of dry shade under a cherry tree.

Aruncus / Goat's beard
◐ (DAMP) H: 1.2M ❄ MAY-JULY

Upright stems with beautifully coloured coppery-red foliage and airy creamy white flowers. **'Horatio'** is less spreading than some varieties, so works for smaller spaces though will form a 1m-plus patch fairly easily. Prefers some dampness. ***A. dioicus* 'Kneiffii'** is more compact with ferny foliage and arching, fluffy cream flowers. It doesn't like to dry out.

Astilbe × *rosea* 'Peach Blossom' / Astilbe 'Peach Blossom'
◐ (DAMP) H: 60CM ❄ JUNE-AUGUST

There are so many different cultivars of astilbe and they are mostly deemed old fashioned, but I reckon they're due a return. It's a strong choice, but the ostrich feather flowers really sing against the ferny foliage. This one has peachy-hued flowers; it's not tall so is good in a planter as long as you keep it moist. **'Venus'** is taller, at 1.2m, and has a candyfloss-pink flowers. It doesn't like dry soil either.

← *Astrantia major* subsp. *involucrata* 'Shaggy' / Masterwort 'Shaggy'
◐ ❦ H: 70CM ❄ JUNE-AUGUST

Astrantias are invaluable for their ability to link up a planting scheme across the garden. It's great for pollinators, too. There are lots of cultivars but 'Shaggy' is one of my favourites for its large green-white flowers. **Gill Richardson Group** has deep red flowers and **'Buckland'** is a good pale pink. All can tolerate dry shade once established, but not deep shade.

Begonia grandis subsp. *evansiana* var. *alba* / White hardy begonia
◐ H: 60CM ❄ JULY-SEPTEMBER

Tropical green foliage with red veins meet pink-white, dainty flowers. Good for most shade and will self-seed (though is prone to collapse). Looks far more hardy than it actually is.

Cenolophium denudatum / Baltic parsley
◐ H: 90CM ❄ JUNE-SEPTEMBER

Essentially a posh, slightly more vertical cow parsley that can take a good bit of shade, though not dry shade. Expect endless frothy cream flowerheads on delicate ferny foliage, and great seedheads. Prefers fertile soil, but isn't overly fussy. Total winner.

Chelidonium majus / Greater celandine

◑ H: 40CM ❄️ MAY-SEPTEMBER

A self-seeder that is particularly good for wildlife gardens. Very pretty pinnate foliage and bright yellow flowers emerge in spring and summer.

Corydalis lutea / Yellow corydalis ↑

● ◑ (DRY) 🌱 H: 30CM ❄️ MAY-SEPTEMBER

Another self-seeder with delicate evergreen foliage and yellow flowers, though these are smaller and neater than greater celandine (*Chelidonium majus*). Pops up in cracks and walls and is good for softening hard lines. **'Blue Heron'** (pictured above) flowers March–September and has remarkably, almost unnaturally intense blue flowers and scented foliage.

Digitalis / Foxglove ↑

◑ 🌱 H: 60CM-1.2M ❄️ MAY-JULY

This genus is another stalwart of the woodland garden. The vertical shape is so useful, especially in dark corners, though foxgloves can take a fair amount of sun as well as shade, they just don't like it too dry. Most are biennials, so they will flower and set seed in their second year if grown from seed, but some, such as **D. × mertonensis** (strawberry foxglove), act more like perennials. There is a huge range of foxgloves to choose from, but these are a few of my favourites. **D. purpurea f. albiflora** is pure white with a statuesque form. **D. purpurea 'Sutton's Apricot'** has soft peach-coloured flowers that work with so many planting palettes and is a little more subtle than f. *albiflora*. **D. purpurea 'Dalmation**

Peach' is a similar colour to 'Sutton's Apricot', but shorter and neater at 60cm; useful for a planter. **D. lutea** is similarly small and neat with the palest of yellow flowers; works beautifully with woodland planting. Strawberry foxglove flowers in July and August in a hue of strawberry-pink smudged with soft gold speckles. It's a mid-height cultivar that looks lovely with grasses and ferns.

Disporum longistylum 'Night Heron' / Chinese fairy bells 'Night Heron' →
● ◐ ⛏ H: 1M ❋ MAY-JUNE

An exotic plant with dark stems, deep purple-green foliage and delicate green-white, bell shaped flowers. Clump-forming, it can tolerate full shade but prefers a bit of warmth.

Euphorbia amygdaloides var. *robbiae* / Mrs Robb's bonnet →
● ◐ (DRY) ⛏ 💧 H: 60CM ❋ APRIL-JUNE

A neat euphorbia that still features the signature foliage and zingy yellow flowers and is happy in shade. As with all euphorbias, be careful when handling as the sap from the stems can burn skin. **E. amygdaloides** is equally good, though smaller and a bit more delicate.

Eurybia divaricata / White wood aster

← *Eurybia divaricata* /
White wood aster

◐ 🌱 H: 60CM ❄ AUGUST-OCTOBER

This features clouds of white, daisy-like flowers on black, wiry stems. It does take a while to establish but then will romp. A really good hardy, late-summer flowerer.

Filipendula palmata / Siberian
meadowsweet

◐ (DAMP) 🌱 H: 1.2M ❄ JULY-AUGUST

Good for moist soils and soils with poor drainage, this statuesque plant has frothy pink-white flowers that pollinators adore. *F. rubra* **'Venusta'** is slightly bigger (growing up to 2m) with candyfloss-pink flowers. You'll definitely need some space, but it is perfect for a bog garden.

← *Geranium phaeum* 'Album' /
Dusky cranesbill 'Album'

● ◐ (DRY) (DAMP) 🌱 H: 75CM ❄ MAY-JUNE

A good option for poor soil. Chalk-white flowers and mounding foliage look great; cut back after flowering for fresh foliage and (fingers crossed) a second flush of flowers. Its beloved by pollinators. **'Raven'** is just as good (pictured). It has beautiful moody purple flowers that can get lost in a border, but that sing in a pot or against a light background.

Geum rivale / Water avens →
◐ (DAMP) H: 40CM ❀ MAY-JULY

A very subtle geum with dusky-pink
and dark orange colouring and unusual
fuzzy seedheads for late-summer
interest. It takes more shade than
cultivated geums and likes damp soil.

Gillenia trifoliata / Bowman's root
◐ H: 1M ❀ JUNE-AUGUST

Such a useful shade plant that, like
so many, isn't as easy as it should be
to find. Sprays of butterfly-like, white
flowers emerge in summer hovering
over green palmate leaves that turn
red in autumn. Good seedheads, too.

Helleborus argutifolius /
Corsican hellebore →
◐ ⚔ ⬥ H: 50CM ❀ JANUARY-MARCH

Not everyone loves this particular
hellebore, but I find its apple-green,
cupped flowers really appealing every
single January. Architectural semi-
evergreen foliage looks good, though
the flowers need to be cut back in early
or mid-summer as they can look untidy.

Hesperis matronalis var. albiflora / Sweet rocket

◑ ⚘ H: 90CM ❄ MAY-JUNE

A short-lived perennial that is usually sown from seed as a biennial. It has pure white, tall flowers from spring that will continue into summer if you deadhead, though do leave some seedheads if you want it to self-seed. Great for pollinators.

Heuchera / Coral bells ↓

◑ ⚘ 💧 H: 30-40CM ❄ MAY-JULY

This genus provides such an amazing variety of unusually coloured rosettes of semi-evergreen foliage, from peach to lime-green, bright red to purple. Small spikes of pollinator-friendly, tiny, bell-shaped flowers are a joy. Some of my favourites are **H. sanguinea 'Coral Petite'**, which has bright green foliage with coral flowers

Helleborus orientalis / Lenten rose ↑

◑ ⚘ H: 30CM ❄ JANUARY-MARCH

There are so many hellebore species in so many hues, from pure white to black-purple via dusky-pink. Long-lasting nodding flowers arrive from late winter and can last into spring. There are too many to list here, but you can't go wrong with the beautiful flowers and evergreen foliage of this classic species among ferns and snowdrops.

Heracleum sphondylium 'Pink Cloud' / Hogweed 'Pink Cloud'

● ◑ ⚘ H: 1.4M ❄ JULY-SEPTEMBER

A cultivated pink hogweed (that's not invasive!) and a recent and welcome discovery for me. I have one in my lightwell, which gets about two hours of direct light, and it looks brilliant. Pollinators are always nearby.

that really pop from May to August. **'White Cloud'** is a lovely white form, while **H. 'Obsidian'** has dark purple-black foliage with creamy-white flowers (pictured opposite). They both flower from June to August.

Hosta 'Devon Green' / Plantain lily
● ◑ (DAMP) 🏺 H: 40CM ❄ JUNE

There is a conspicuous lack of hostas on this list – I don't tend to grow them because the competition with the slugs and snails is too much for me. 'Devon Green' doesn't have a huge leaf and is not as showy as many other hostas, but it's a lovely green with distinctive ribbing. It works well structurally and texturally in so many planting combinations (if it doesn't get eaten first). A gardener I know coats the rim of her impressive hosta pots with an unholy mixture of vaseline and coarse sea salt, which seems to work for her.

Iris sibirica 'Perry's Blue' / Siberian iris
◑ (DAMP) H: 80CM ❄ MAY-JUNE

A very pretty iris with pale blue flowers marked with white. Prefers damp soil, so is perfect for a bog garden or at the edge of water. Strong, strap-like foliage provides structure after flowering.

Lamium orvala / Balm-leaved red deadnettle ↑
● ◑ (DRY) H: 70CM ❄ APRIL-AUGUST

Green foliage and reddish-purple flowerheads provide a great show and there isn't much better than watching a bee wiggling itself right into the flowers. **L. album** (pictured) is smaller and neater with pure white flowers that are just as popular with the bees. For more deadnettles see page 96.

Lamprocapnos spectabilis 'Alba' / White bleeding heart

● ◐ (DAMP) ✿ H: 60CM ❀ APRIL-JUNE

Large, arching stems hold distinctive pure white flowers aloft over foliage that dies back in midsummer but comes back reliably each year. It's said to dislike drying out, but mine does well in a planter without excessive watering.

Lunaria annua var. albiflora / White-flowered honesty

◐ (DRY) H: 75CM ❀ JUNE-SEPTEMBER

Not a perennial, but a lovely shade-loving biennial with white flowers that pop in the shade. Translucent papery seedheads develop in autumn. It freely self-seeds, so has snuck into this list. **L. rediviva** reaches about 1m tall and flowers May–August and is the perennial species; it also has wonderful oval seedheads.

Mathiasella bupleuroides 'Green Dream' / Mathiasella 'Green Dream'

◐ H: 1M ❀ APRIL-JUNE

A statuesque, architectural wonder. Semi-evergreen, grey-green foliage with long stems holding nodding jade-green, bell-shaped flowers that turn pink in late summer and autumn. It is monocarpic, which means the plant will die after flowering, but self-seeds first.

Meconopsis cambrica / Welsh poppy

● ◐ ✿ H: 40CM ❀ JUNE-SEPTEMBER

Welsh poppies range from yellow to deep orange and are prolific self-seeders – they will pop up everywhere once you introduce them. They are so, so pretty and can unite planting across a garden if you have sunny and shady borders.

Melanoselinum decipiens / Black parsley

◐ ✿ ♠ H: 2M ❀ APRIL-JUNE

A short-lived but really striking exotic, architectural perennial that is toxic despite its common name. In a sheltered courtyard, side return or balcony its foliage is evergreen. Give it a couple of years and it will produce large, pale pink, umbel flowers. It is monocarpic (like mathiasella opposite).

Myrrhis odorata / Sweet cicely

◐ ✿ H: 80CM ❀ APRIL-JUNE

I plant this under my roses but it goes anywhere. The ferny foliage and lacy white flowers are all edible, and are traditionally used to sweeten stewed fruit – a few leaves in a salad works really well.

Top left Lamprocapnos spectabilis 'Alba'
Top right Mathiasella bupleuroides 'Green Dream' **Bottom left** Meconopsis cambrica
Bottom right Melanoselinum decipiens

Nicotiana sylvestris / **Woodland tobacco plant** ↑
● ◐ 🌱 H:1.5M ❊ OCTOBER

Tall, towering and elegant with white, trumpet flowers that smell amazing at dusk, this short-lived perennial is usually grown as an annual, so seeds are commonly available. *N. langsdorffii* is a soft, lime-green annual cultivar. Put both in pots so you can move them around to get the sun or place at the back of a partially shaded border. Pollinators love them.

Omphalodes cappadocica 'Cherry Ingram' / **Navelwort**
◐ (DAMP) H:25CM ❊ MARCH-APRIL

The brightest blue, forget-me-not-type flowers and bright green foliage make this plant sing. It doesn't like drying out and slugs do like to get involved, but I've seen it pop up under a tree where

the soil is like dust, so it's always worth taking a punt.

Paris polyphylla
● ◐ H:90CM ❊ MAY-JUNE

Exotic foliage and slightly alien-like spidery flowers make this one worth searching for. It's an ideal perennial for deep shade, but is tender so will need shelter to survive the winter. It also loves humus-rich soil.

Persicaria / **Knotweed** ↑ ↗
◐ (DAMP) H:60-90CM ❊ JULY-SEPTEMBER

These are brilliant plants for adding movement to a border and are really good for pollinators. They definitely won't tolerate full shade, but they are happy in dappled or part shade. I love their sometimes unruly slender stems and flowers. They tend to bulk up over a couple of years and do look better in

Pimpinella major 'Rosea' / Pink greater burnet saxifrage

◐ (DAMP) 🌱 H: 1M ❄ MAY-JUNE

Essentially a pinkish-mauve cow parsley (*Anthriscus sylvestris*) with a great name and fantastic height. What could be nicer?

Podophyllum versipelle 'Spotty Dotty' / Mayapple 'Spotty Dotty'

● ◐ (DAMP) 🌱 H: 40CM ❄ APRIL-MAY

Startlingly unusual, large, mottled foliage makes this a Marmite plant but one I like. It has red flowers with an unpleasant scent, which are usually hidden under the leaves. Likes damp, humus-rich soil, but happy in a planter.

Polygonatum / Solomon's seal

● ◐ (DAMP) 🌱 ❄ APRIL-JUNE

This genus is excellent for shade, and many species are drought-tolerant once established – though do note that all are poisonous. *P.* × *hybridum* reaches 1m with arching stems of drooping, creamy, bell-shaped flowers and dark pairs of leaves. *P. odoratum* is just 40cm tall and is less arching, but is scented. *P. verticillatum* **'Rubrum'** is an elegant cultivar with narrow leaves and pink-mauve bell flowers. I have this in a pot next to lots of different ferns in a really shady spot and the foliage contrasts very nicely.

drifts, but they can also work in large planters. There are so many interesting cultivars, but these are my favourites (with a few more selected in the Ground Cover list on page 97). *P. virginiana* **var. *filiformis* 'Lance Corporal'** has bright green foliage with a dark red chevron flash. Lots of dark red flower spikes emerge from late summer to early autumn. It spreads around so keep an eye on it, though this one is good for planters if you want to keep it contained. *P. amplexicaulis* **'Alba'** has white flowers and, at 90cm, is a usefully tall see-through plant (pictured opposite). Once established, it's low maintenance and beautiful with grasses or Japanese anemones (*A.* × *hybrida*). **'Blackfield'** has deep red flowers, while **'Pink Elephant'** (pictured above) is more compact with candy-pink flowers. This works in planters too.

Pulmonaria 'Blue Ensign' / Lungwort 'Blue Ensign'

◑ ❦ H: 30CM ✿ APRIL-MAY

A fantastic early-spring plant with startling gentian-blue flowers and silvery lung-shaped foliage. Very bee-friendly. **'Sissinghurst White'** is a white variety, though flowers start off pale pink, with soft silver-spotted foliage. **Opal** has pale blue flowers with silvery leaves and is good at lighting up darker areas of the garden.

Ranunculus aconitifolius / Aconite buttercup

◑ H: 90CM ✿ APRIL-JUNE

Lovely white buttercup flowers on tall, slender, branching stems – this one is ideal for early-summer flowers.

Rodgersia pinnata 'Superba'

◑ (DAMP) ❦ H: 1M ✿ MAY-JULY

'Superba' has excellent, large, deeply divided architectural foliage that starts off bronze before turning green, as well as sprays of vibrant pink flowers in summer, which also look good once they've gone over. You can just about grow this in a large pot, but it likes damp soil so place the pot in a deep sauce of water. It needs a bit of shelter too. **R. podophylla** is taller (1.5m) with creamy flowers and palmate bronze leaves that turn green by summer. It flowers later from July to August.

Sanguisorba officinalis / Greater burnet ↑

◑ (DAMP) ❦ H: 1.5M ✿ JULY-SEPTEMBER

Sanguisorba definitely needs some light, but it is worth a shot unless you've got deep shade. I love its dark red, bottlebrush flowerheads on wavy, thin stems and delicate foliage. It is clump forming and long flowering but needs moisture-retentive soil and staking. Admittedly, I don't usually get round to it and it tends to flop around my garden unless held up by useful uprights like the grass Calamagrostis × acutiflora 'Karl Foerster' and thalictrums. **S. tenuifolia 'Pink Elephant'** has the most incredible fuzzy flowers: they start off dark pink and gradually lighten and drop down – they look good at the back of a border or in drifts. If you don't have the space, go for **S. 'Tanna'**, a compact variety.

Selinum wallichianum / Wallich milk parsley
◑ H: 1M ❄ JULY-SEPTEMBER

A great umbellifer with strong structure and frothy cow-parsley flowers and foliage. Reliable (as long as it doesn't get too dry) and perfect with thalictrums (see opposite). Excellent seedheads, too.

Silene vulgaris / Bladder campion ↑
◑ (DRY) H: 60CM ❄ JULY-AUGUST

A really unusual, semi-evergreen wildflower that features in a lot of my window boxes, though does get a bit straggly in them. I always think the flowers look like little Victorian pie-crust collars on fat bottoms! **S. fimbriata** (fringed campion) is equally lovely, but even more frilly, taller and a bit less straggly.

Tellima grandiflora / Fringe cups
● ◑ H: 60CM ❄ APRIL-JUNE

One of my favourite spring plants. Slender stems are fringed with tiny cup flowers that are initially green-white before turning pink. Can take a fair bit of shade and will work planted under trees. If you can find it, go for the scented **Odorata Group**.

Thalictrum / Meadow rue ↑
◑ (DAMP) H: 1.7M ❄ JUNE-SEPTEMBER

Thalictrum is a genus of plants and there are many brilliant species. **T. aquilegiifolium** has pretty pink fluffy flowerheads, while **T. delavayi** (Chinese meadow rue) is a total stunner (pictured). Tall, elegant and with foliage that's almost like an evergreen maidenhair fern; it also has beautifully see-through flowers like droplets of rain. Young plants may need staking (or planting near supporting plants), but they reliably come back every year. *T. delavayi* **'Album'** is a beautiful white variety.

Tiarella / Foam flower
● ◑ H: 50CM ❄ MAY-JULY

Another generous genus that encompasses many wonderful species and varieties. **'Spring Symphony'** and **'Pink Skyrocket'** are both pretty and reasonably easy to find. Great in pots and planters or planted around ferns in borders. The fuzzy pink flowers are long lasting and keep coming back with diligent deadheading.

Tricyrtis formosana / Toad lily
● ◑ (DAMP) H: 80CM
❄ SEPTEMBER-OCTOBER

A useful plant for late-season colour and interest that has dainty, pink-purple, speckled, lily-like flowers on tall stems. It prefers a little damp if possible.

Trollius chinensis 'Golden Queen' / Globeflower 'Golden Queen'
◑ (DAMP) H: 90CM ❄ JUNE-JULY

As a damp meadow flower, this one likes a moisture-retentive soil – if that's what you've got, you'll find these rich, golden, globe flowers total winners. *T. europaeus* is a touch shorter and has soft yellow, equally striking flowers in May and June.

Uvularia grandiflora / Merry bells
● ◑ (DAMP) H: 70CM ❄ APRIL-MAY

Bright green foliage in spring with dangling, nodding, yellow flowers with twisted petals. A good option if you have damp shade.

Valeriana officinalis / Common valerian
◑ H: 1.5M ❄ JULY-AUGUST

This long-flowering plant is underused, which is curious as it's so attractive and useful, and beloved by pollinators. It works in a similar way to *Verbena bonariensis*, in that it is stately and see-through so is good for adding depth. The downsides are it self-seeds a lot (though you could just see this as free plants) and doesn't smell particularly good, so not ideal for the vase.

Veronicastrum virginicum 'Album' / Culver's root
◑ H: 1.4M ❄ JUNE-AUGUST

Tall, elegant, wafty, white spires provide some see-through structure in summer and still look good once the flowers have gone over. It does need a bit of space once established as it creates a more striking impression planted in drifts. Alternatives include **'Fascination'**, which is a lilac cultivar, and **'Challenger'**, which is pale pink.

Top left *Tiarella* Top right *Uvularia grandiflora*
Bottom left and right *Valeriana officinalis*

Planting combinations / For pots and borders

←

Athyrium filix-femina,
Hydrangea petiolaris,
Polygonatum × *hybridum,*
Anemone × *hybrida*
'Honorine Jobert', *Hosta*
'Devon Green'
These steps get a couple
of hours of sun in the early
evening during summer;
they were really grotty
when we moved in, but a
million pots (and snails)
later, and they have
completely transformed
the view from the kitchen.
I move the pots around
depending on what is in
flower, but foliage is what's
most important here.

←

Geranium robertianum,
Helleborus orientalis
This is the evergreen
foliage of a hellebore and
a self-seeded herb Robert
showing that nature often
creates far better planting
plans than we do.

→

Rosa **The Lady of the**
Lake, *Myrrhis odorata*
and *Athyrium filix-femina*
A really pretty
combination. This spot
does get a fair bit of sun
in the late afternoon, but
I've planted these plants
together in other gardens
with far less light and they
work just as well.

Trees

When investing in a tree, be sure to check its ultimate height and width as well as the growth rate. Many trees are slow growing, which may or may not work for you. Trees can be pleached or espaliered when space is limited, which can look particularly effective against brick walls. Adding trees to your garden does add shade – it can be seasonal, dappled or dense shade – but they also add structure and are great for wildlife. Multi-stem specimens work well in small spaces because you can see through them; note that many shrubs, such as viburnums or osmanthus, can be used as multi-stem small trees if they are correctly pruned (removing their lower branches can reveal a good structural form and add light). Lastly, don't be put off by the height – compact gardens and balconies only look smaller with a small lollipop tree in the corner rather than a taller spreading tree.

← *Acer palmatum* / Japanese maple

A genus with so many elegant trees and shrubs to choose from. Acers can be tricky: their foliage is often easily scorched and they need a sheltered spot. They are slow growing, which makes them fairly expensive, but also able to survive in pots. In general, the dark red ones can take more sun than the bright green ones. Smaller ones look good among other foliage on a balcony, but they don't like wind exposure, so only include if you can offer some protection. **'Bi Ho'** and **'Dissectum'** both reach about 2m. 'Bi Ho' is an unusual cultivar with a stunning golden bark and salmon-pink leaves, and 'Dissectum' has a delicate, highly divided leaf with a weeping habit. **'Going Green'** reaches 5m and I love the lime-green of its foliage in spring. It turns bright green before becoming orange-yellow in autumn. The bare stems are a vivid green in winter. Finally, **'Kagiri-nishiki'** grows to 4m and is an unusual variegated cultivar with green leaves lined with pink.

Amelanchier lamarckii / Snowy mespilus

A multi-stem, snowy mespilus is a go-to for small gardens. It has a lovely natural shape, year-round interest with picture-perfect blossom and dark purple berries (edible to us and the birds) and good autumn colour. It's also tolerant of pollution. A total winner.

Arbutus unedo / Strawberry tree
H: 6M

Very useful evergreen tree with white bell-shaped flowers followed by bright red-orange edible fruits (if it gets some sun) that look like pom-poms.

Chamaerops humilis / Dwarf fan palm
◐ ♦ H: 2.5M

Not for the faint-hearted, this tropical-looking palm has sharp thorns and does require regular pruning. It's brilliant at creating an exotic vibe and the more shade the more elongated and, to me, elegant it becomes.

Cornus alternifolia 'Argentea' / Silver pagoda dogwood
◐ ⚱ H: 2.5M ✿ JUNE

A very striking tiered tree with variegated leaves and white flowers. It's slow growing, so good for small gardens or an extra-large pot.

Cryptomeria japonica 'Globosa Nana' / Japanese cedar 'Globosa Nana'
◐ ⚱ ♦ H: 50CM

A covetable evergreen dwarf conifer. It's slow growing, but will form a round, tactile, fluffy mound. Likes moisture-retentive soil.

Eriobotrya japonica / Loquat
◐ ⚱ ♦ H: 6M

Useful, small and unfussy, this tree also produces apricot-like fruit (if you're lucky). It has large, dark green, glossy leaves and likes a sheltered spot.

Malus / Crab apple
◐ ⚱ H: 7M ✿ MARCH–APRIL

Lots of crab apple trees work in small to medium gardens. For me, **'Evereste'** has particularly attractive pink blossom that turns white, as well as good fruit. It's also pollution tolerant.

Schefflera actinophylla / Queensland umbrella tree ↑
◐ ⚱ ♦ H: 4M

An exotic, architectural, multi-stem tree with elegant, leathery foliage. It does appreciate a bit of shelter, but is fairly hardy, especially in mild city gardens.

Tetrapanax papyrifer 'Rex' / Chinese rice-paper plant 'Rex'
◐ ⚱ ♦ H: 3M

Huge (up to 1m across) eye-catching foliage makes this a remarkable plant. Works in a variety of planting styles, is fast growing and very hardy. It may need tidying up, especially after a cold winter, but it is reliable. If it's in a really sheltered spot it will be evergreen.

Edibles

There are plenty of vegetables, soft-leaved herbs and fruits you can grow in varying amounts of shade. If your light is really limited, you may get a reduced harvest or plants may take a little longer to fruit, but most edibles need some shade throughout the day. Herbs such as mint are much more manageable (spreading with less vigour) in lower light and generally edible plants are slower to bolt. Planting smaller crops like salad leaves, herbs and radishes in pots that you can move around to catch the sun is useful.

Many edibles can be grown as ornamentals too: rhubarb foliage gives a jungle vibe, hops and currants can be trained along a wall for interest, wild strawberries make good ground cover, bolted herbs and brassicas produce pollinator-friendly flowers and salad leaves come in all shapes and colours.

Whatever spot you have, make sure your soil is as good as possible. Add lots of well-rotted manure and mulch it well. The need to water is reduced in the shade, unless you are planting beneath trees or in pots, but snails and slugs may be a bigger issue.

For an area in full shade, but with some diffused light (such as a tall-walled courtyard) you can grow: gooseberries, blackberries, currants, brassicas, salad leaves and herbs such as mint and lemon balm.

For an area in moderate shade (such as a side return or beneath a north-facing wall) add to the above list: root vegetables, kale, spinach, chard, rhubarb, apples, wild strawberries, loganberries, raspberries, Japanese wineberries (pictured below), parsley, chives, chervil and angelica.

For an area in light, dappled or part shade (such as under deciduous trees), add the following: potatoes, peas, beans, carrots, broccoli, celery, leeks, radishes, wasabi, oregano, sweet cicely, tarragon and fruit trees including pear and cherry.

Above A section of the balcony as seen from the street.
Opposite The view of the balcony from inside the living room

I think Eelke's balcony is a masterclass in planting a small space with large foliage plants. It always stops me in my tracks whenever I cycle past it. The balcony is on the ground floor and has a north-west facing dual-aspect. The north-facing side gets an hour of sun and the west-facing side a few hours of late-afternoon sun in summer. There's further shade from the trees in the park opposite as well as the balconies above. As the balcony is on the ground floor, a seating area would feel very exposed to the street, so filling it with plants provides extra privacy. It does cut down the light received inside the flat, but the view is easily worth it.

This garden didn't evolve, but was planned by Eelke from the start, as he knew that it was too exposed to ever sit in. The contrasting foliage is both lush and dynamic with a number of unusual plants.

'I negotiated in the purchase lease that I was able to install taps on each balcony and terrace for easy watering. I made the steel planters myself, which are big enough for trees. I wanted a variety of leaf size and colour, and no flowers due to the lack of light. My biggest joy is looking at it from the outside: it is quite a sight when you compare it with the rest of the buildings in the street. A green heaven in a rather urban setting.'

Shade gardens /
Eelke Jan Bles

04

Care
Learn to support your plants and help them thrive

A garden is never finished. I don't mean this in a bad way, it's an intrinsic part of the process of creating something living. The more time you spend noticing your plants, planning new plantings, looking to the future as well as tending to the present, the more you will gain from your garden. Finding five minutes a day to step outside and see what's going on, what's changed, what's happy and what's not is a therapeutic way of unwinding and building a relationship with the space you have created. It could be first thing in the morning with a cup of tea or at dusk when the swifts are wheeling above you.

Unfortunately, there isn't really any such thing as a low-maintenance garden unless you are looking at a square of astroturf, but choosing plants that are happy in the conditions you give them should reduce the amount of time spent looking after them. In my garden there is quite a lot of 'survival of the fittest' going on; I don't tend to feed plants in the borders (apart from roses and fruit and veg), because I want them to survive in the conditions I have, and I don't use any form of pesticides, so it's fairly wild and woolly. But some care is of course essential and enjoyable.

Supporting your plants

A few simple gardening practices will give you a healthy, thriving garden.

PLANTING

The ideal time to get planting is autumn. The ground should still be warm and many plants have finished flowering so they can concentrate on putting roots down. Spring is good too; it just means the plants won't be as established by summer. A newly planted plant will need extra care and attention until it's established, especially if it has come from a nursery where it has lived in cosseted conditions. This might mean giving it a really good water once it's planted and making sure it's well watered in its first year. And it might also mean keeping an eye on it for a season or so to make sure it has room to grow and isn't being swamped by neighbouring plants.

Many plants bought from nurseries can be potbound – this is when the plant has outgrown the pot and the rootball has become congested. If I've bought a plant in this condition, I normally soak its roots for an hour or so in a bucket of water, then tease out some of the matted roots before planting. You can do this by rubbing the sides of the rootball with your fingertips until the finer roots break, and then loosen the roots at the bottom. If it has a really good rootball, you can divide it into a couple of plants – just make sure you have growing points and roots on each section (see page 144). Don't be afraid of damaging the plant; this process helps it form new roots that spread out in the soil, rather than staying in a clump. If your soil is poor, add a good handful of compost or manure to the hole so that the roots find nutrients.

STAKING

Tall plants like Chinese meadow rue (*Thalictrum delavayi*) and sanguisorba often need staking to prevent them from collapsing. Staking needs to happen early on in the plant's growth – usually early spring – so that it's in place as the plant is growing and will be disguised by foliage later in the year. Staking once the plant is tall and floppy rarely works, though in all honesty this is usually when I get round to it.

Supporting climbers Most climbers need support and, as with staking, it's easier to add this before they have shot two metres above your head. Some climbers, like ivy or climbing hydrangea (*H. petiolaris*) are self-supporting – or self-clinging – so don't need any support. Others, like chocolate vine (*Akebia quinata*) or hops (*Humulus lupulus*), have lots of fast-growing tendrils that wrap themselves around anything, so need something to clamber up, but not a lot of tying in. Roses, on the other hand,

need careful tying in through the growing season.

Check your climber's needs before investing in a support. In general, I find training wire with metal vine eyes works best for walls as it's neat and unfussy, but you can also use a trellis or existing fence. There are also obelisks, nets, pergolas and more on the market – and you can always fashion your own stand-alone supports using hazel, willow or birch. Another piece of excellent advice I'm bad at following is always keeping a handful of garden twine to hand so that you can tie in tendrils when you see them rather than thinking you'll do it later and forgetting instantly.

FEEDING

If you have healthy soil, rich in nutrients and organisms, you don't usually need to add fertiliser, which works to boost the nutrient content of the soil. Sometimes, plants will show signs of deficiency – often yellowing leaves or some other discolouration – and may need some extra help. Container-grown plants, fruit, vegetables and very hungry plants (such as roses) will need some feed.

Compound fertilisers These contain three main macronutrients: nitrogen (N), phosphorus (P) and potassium (K). These nutrients perform different, important functions to aid plant growth. Not all fertilisers

A bouquet of comfrey (*Symphytum*) leaves

Phosphorus Supporting roots and shoots growth, phosphorus is good for helping plants to establish.

Potassium This helps to boost flower and fruit growth, as well as for general plant growth and hardiness.

Seaweed fertiliser is a natural and sustainable feed that avoids the animal byproducts that other fertilisers (such as blood, fish and bone) can have.

Compost You can make your own compost with the help of a compost heap or bin (if you have space) and use this as a mulch on top of your beds or you can gently dig it in – it will improve the structure of your soil and add essential nutrients.

Comfrey Rich in potash, potassium and nitrogen, comfrey leaves can easily be made into a fertilising tea.

have the same proportions of these nutrients, but the quantifiable balance of the three should be clearly marked on the packaging. For example, the organic garden feed I'm looking at now has a ratio of 5:2:5, which means it has over twice as much nitrogen (N) and potassium (K) than phosphorus (P).

Nitrogen This is used primarily to boost leaf growth and is especially useful if you are growing vegetables.

Harvest the leaves from late April, wearing gloves. Remove coarse stems and flowers and then tear into pieces. Fill a non-metal bucket with a lid (or have something you can cover the bucket with) until it's loosely packed with the leaves. Weigh them down with a large stone or brick and then cover them with water and the lid. After a minimum of three weeks they will have broken down, with the help of an occasional stir. Strain off the impressively disgusting-smelling brown liquid from the sludge of foliage.

According to pioneering gardener Charles Dowding, you can also make this without water by just adding the leaves to a large terracotta pot with a single drainage hole. Place the pot in a larger plastic bucket and place a heavy lid on top, so that no rain can get in. It's a slower process (around 8–12 weeks), but the leaves are broken down by existing micro-organisms and the resulting mixture will filter into the plastic bucket and it doesn't smell.

To use comfrey tea as a general feed, dilute it 1:10 with water. Then water your plants with it ideally using a watering can with a fine rose. You can water the plants' leaves as a foliage feed and/or the soil around the base of the plants. If you have access to lots of comfrey, you can continue adding fresh leaves to the brew.

MULCHING

Mulch is a top dressing, most often some form of organic matter, that you can add to beds to improve or support soil structure and health. If you have sandy soil, mulch can help replace the nutrients washed away by rain; if you have heavy clay soil, it can improve the drainage.

Composted bark chips, broken-down leafmould, mushroom compost, straw, manure and grass clippings can all be used as mulch. I also leave my garden fairly messy over winter. Allowing plants to die back rather than cutting them

gives you a natural mulch, which feeds the soil and provides food and habitat for birds and insects. It saves a lot of time, plus I'm a big fan of seedheads.

Mulch acts as a barrier, so rather than digging it in just lay it carefully on top of your soil, leaving a little room around any plant stems. Do this in spring and again in early winter (if necessary) to improve the soil's condition and drainage, as well as act as a weed suppressant (though you do need to weed first). Shade plants tend to require less mulching than those in a sunny position. A layer of about 7cm is usually fine (compared to the 10–15cm of mulch you typically add to a bed in full sun). Once the mulch is on, the worms will do the work for you, taking it deeper into the soil. By pulling it into the soil, they improve the soil structure and make it more free-draining.

Don't use peat or peat-based compost or fertilisers. Peat is the partially decomposed matter of plants that grow in boggy areas and has traditionally been added to compost to help retain moisture. However, there are many good reasons not to use it. Global peat bogs absorb large amounts of carbon – twice as much as all the world's forests – and as we erode the bogs the carbon is released back into the atmosphere. Peat bogs are also a non-renewable natural resource that take thousands of years to form. And finally, they are home to a huge amount of wildlife.

Deadheading and pruning

Early-summer flowerers, such as lady's mantle (*Alchemilla mollis*), lungwort (*Pulmonaria*), bleeding heart (*Lamprocapnos spectabilis*) and hardy geraniums, benefit from being cut right back in late June after flowering. It not only makes them look neater, but vitally it also encourages new foliage growth, stops seed growth and in some cases encourages a second flush of flowers in late summer. You can be quite tough and cut them back to a few centimetres from the ground (pictured, right).

Plants such as tiarellas, astrantias, heucheras and some roses benefit from regular deadheading to encourage new blooms throughout their flowering season. For roses, cut back flowering stems to just above a new bud or leaf, rather than just nipping the head off (see image on page 145). For rambling roses, rather than deadheading each individual bloom, cut back the whole cluster just above a new leaf.

Not all climbers need pruning and advice will vary depending on cultivars and varieties. For example, always check which of the three groups your clematis is in before attacking with secateurs, as some flower on new growth and others on the previous season's growth. Climbing hydrangeas (*H. petiolaris*)

Above Brown fern foliage can be trimmed
Opposite Cut flowering stems to a new leaf

can take some gentle pruning after flowering, but if you cut it all back hard you'll have reduced flowering the following year.

I leave the dried flowerheads on shrub hydrangeas (*H. paniculata* and *H. aborescens*) — they are good for wildlife, protect any new, tender growth, plus they give great winter interest. You can cut them back in early spring — they can take a fair bit of pruning — and I usually take stems back to the first pair of healthy buds about 30cm from the ground. Oak-leaved hydrangeas (*H. quercifolia*) don't really need any pruning.

Ferns often develop brown crispy foliage and this should be trimmed off before, or as, the new foliage starts to appear. If you haven't got around to this in time (as clearly I haven't here) you can still trim these parts off — it will allow more air around the new green growth and encourages more foliage.

Late summer The end of the summer season can see gardens and window boxes start to look pretty tatty, especially if there has been little sun and a lot of wind and rain. Even at this late stage, tall plants can still be staked. But if they've fallen over or are too far gone, cut them right back. Dead, diseased or half-munched foliage can be trimmed and this is a particularly good time to deadhead any big self-seeders such as valerian or Welsh poppies (*Meconopsis cambrica*). You can also thin out anything that looks like it's taking over — persicarias, hardy geraniums and grasses love to overtake everything else in my garden.

DIVIDING

Dividing a perennial is a simple method of propagation and gives you new plants to replant in your garden, or if you don't have the room for the extra plant it gives you free plants to give away. Division simply means separating the parent plant into two or more smaller sections, creating more plants and encouraging new growth and vigour in the original plant.

Lots of perennials start to lose a bit of vigour after a few years — if you

notice a lack of growth in the middle of the clump or the flowers and/or leaves are smaller than they used to be, it's often a sign that the plant needs some rejuvenation and will benefit from being divided. Division works for a wide range of plants. The general instructions below should help, but I've also detailed different methods for different groups of plants.

Dividing can be done at any time, as long as the plant is dormant. For the majority of plants, the dormant period is autumn, but do note that for spring-flowering plants such as brunnera, it's best to divide once they have finished flowering, and for late-summer-flowering plants such as astrantias or grasses divide in spring. In all instances it's best to do this on a cool day and, if in spring, once the risk of frost has passed and the ground has started to warm up.

Always dig the plant up gently with a fork, working around the perimeter, then remove as much soil as you can from the roots so you can see the rootball clearly and identify where you want to make a divide. You can give the stems and foliage a trim at this point so that the plant concentrates on putting its roots down in its new home. Depending on the size of the

Anemone × hybrida 'Honorine Jobert' and *Persicaria amplexicaulis* 'Alba' can be divided

plant and density of the rootball, the tools you can use to do this task include two large forks back to back, a saw, a knife (Japanese hori-hori knives are excellent for this) or your hands.

Each section should contain a good portion of roots and stems at the top. You can trim the old roots back to 10–15cm to encourage the growth of new roots. Once you have made your divisions and removed any dead bits of foliage or stem, dig a hole with enough space for the roots to spread, add a little compost, plant your new plant and water in thoroughly.

Mat-forming Ground-cover plants such as sweet violet (*Viola odorata*) or sweet woodruff (*Galium odoratum*) tend to have mat-forming roots and are the easiest to divide. Gently dig up each mat with a hand fork and pull the plant apart with your hands. If it's early spring or autumn, trim the foliage by half before replanting and letting each division concentrate on putting roots down.

Clump-forming Perennials like astrantias, lungwort (*Pulmonaria*), bleeding hearts (*Lamprocapnos spectabilis*) or hostas are clump-forming, which means they tend to be compact plants with growth that comes up from the centre or crown (a crown is the area where the stems join the root). Again, dig up gently either in early spring or after flowering, and gently pull apart so that each division has a good-sized section of root.

Woody crowns Heucheras and geraniums have woody crowns – it's easy to identify when these need dividing as they stop flowering in the middle or just come back with less vigour each year. Once you have dug the plant out, you may need a knife to cut it into sections. It helps to trim the leaves and water well before replanting.

Runners Japanese anemones (*A. × hybrida*) and shuttlecock fern (*Matteuccia struthiopteris*) send out underground runners. Dig up the small young plants that you see around the parent and pot these up or replant.

Grasses Most grasses are happy to be divided. Depending on the size of the plant, you may well need a knife or a saw to cut through the rootball – an established *Calamagrostis × acutiflora* 'Karl Foerster' is a good example. But a good clump of wood melic (*Melica uniflora*) can usually be split by hand.

Ferns Most ferns are also happy to be split, with the exception of the Japanese painted fern (*Athyrium niponicum* var. *pictum*). Wood ferns (*Dryopteris*) and aspleniums have a central crown – you can see the curled fronds around the growing points – so to divide these cut the crown into good-sized sections and make sure each section has a decent bit of root.

Polypodiums have rhizomes: once you've removed the soil you can see where they send roots off, so you gently pull off a bit of rhizome with roots attached and replant.

Hellebores It's worth waiting a few years until hellebores have formed sizeable clumps before dividing. They seed everywhere and they are promiscuous, so unless you have just one cultivar, you never know what the seedlings will become. Dividing is the only way to be sure of getting new plants in the colour you want.

Most hellebore foliage is evergreen, so early autumn is a good time to divide them if you know where they are. Otherwise you can always try to do it after they have finished flowering. Wear gloves as hellebores have a sap that can irritate your skin. Dig carefully around the plant, remove it and brush away as much soil as you can so that you can see the roots, specifically where the plant stems meet the main root – which is a rhizome – at the crown. You can cut this into sections with a sharp knife or good secateurs. You want each section of the rhizome to have one or more stems and some small roots. Plant out straight away, and if you have a number of sections keep them in a bucket of water so they don't dry out while you're planting.

The process of dividing a soft shield fern (*Polystichum setiferum*) by cutting the crown into two sections with a knife

Container care

Planting in containers does mean you have to pay a little more attention to plant care, particularly when it comes to watering and feeding. The compost in pots has a finite quantity of nutrients and once the plants have used these up they will start to lose vigour. If you have a container full of plants, it's best to replace the top few centimetres of soil every year, and completely replace it every 2–3 years, depending on the size of the pot. If you are replacing all the soil, give the container a clean at the same time. You can repot the plant into the same pot, or pot it on into a different or larger container.

Repotting Try to only repot plants when they are dormant, usually in autumn. Ease the plant from the pot – this is not always easy, especially if it's been in the same pot for some time, so be patient. Then gently brush the soil from around the roots with your fingers. If it's looking particularly pot-bound (this is when the plant's roots have become congested) you may want to gently rootprune it. This simply means trimming some of the fine, white roots and any dead-looking roots until the rootball is reduced by up to one third. You can then fill the pot with fresh compost, replace the plant and make sure you pack compost in down the sides so that it is securely planted. Always water well after repotting.

Fertilising I give all my containers a good feed at the start of the growing season in spring and periodically throughout the growing season until they start to die back (see page 140). If you are growing perennials, you may need to divide them every few years to maintain their health and ensure they have space to grow (see page 144).

Watering This is probably the time-consuming part of container gardening as it is a job that must be done regularly. Rain is the best kind of watering (minerals found in mains water, especially in hard-water areas, can lower the pH of your soil, which may prevent the plant gathering nutrients), but if you have a densely planted pot it's unlikely much rain will reach the soil, as the foliage acts as an umbrella. Rainy days rarely mean a break from watering pots.

To improve water retention in your pots, you can mulch the tops with a decorative mulch like gravel, which will help lock in moisture. You can also place your containers on drip trays that collect water – this means excess water is saved and can be gradually absorbed by the roots when needed. However, do be careful with this – not all plants want to be sitting in a saucer of water.

A very small snail munching on my persicaria

You need diversity of planting to increase diversity of insects. Not all bugs are bad

PESTS

Shade plants are not affected by pests more than any other plants, but cool, damp conditions are perfect for slugs and snails, so there is no getting away from them in a shade garden. There are lots of tricks to keep them away from your plants, although I'm not convinced how well any of them work. I just grit my teeth and leave them to it – life is too short to be emptying slug beer traps.

Powdery mildew can affect plants such as roses, begonias and amelanchiers. This is a fungus that looks exactly as it sounds and, apart from looking horrible, it can absorb nutrients from the plant and block the chloroplasts, which can restrict growth. Humidity can exacerbate the issue, so, if you can, thin out any plants that have powdery mildew so that more air can circulate. Cut off any diseased foliage and cut anything back that will allow a little more sunlight to reach the affected plants. You can also spray the leaves with a mixture of bicarbonate of soda and water: just add two tablespoons of bicarbonate of soda to 500ml of water.

The sassafras tree at the
centre has beautifully
shaped foliage and people
are always trying to buy
it, but it's one of the few
plants that are not for sale

Shade gardens / Linda

This tiny courtyard (my part-time shop) is a
constant and evolving experiment to see what
will survive and what won't. It gets a couple of
hours of direct sun on the south-facing wall
in summer, otherwise it gets indirect light
for most of the day. The north-facing wall
receives no light and features a cheap hanging
basket with a hart's tongue fern (*Asplenium
scolopendrium*) and a self-seeded white herb
Robert (*Geranium robertianum* 'Album') – it's
one of my favourite things and lives side
by side with a large tree fern (*Dicksonia
antarctica*) and a climbing hydrangea
(*H. petiolaris*). A 'greenhouse' made from a
collection of old metal doors (two were already
in the yard) lines the back wall and houses
what I grandly like to call my pelargonium
collection. The only thing that's missing is
some water, but I'm plotting a small pond –
I just need to find the right receptacle.

Page numbers in *italic* indicate a caption to an illustration; those in **bold** indicate a particular garden or main entry.

Nurseries in the UK

These are just some of the nurseries that I really like. Not all of them do mail order and some have limited opening times, but it's worth perusing their plant lists for inspiration alone. Some of them also have open days and run courses.

Architectural Plants
architecturalplants.com

Beth Chatto's Plants and Gardens
bethchatto.co.uk

Burncoose Nurseries
burncoose.co.uk

Edulis
edulis.co.uk

Great Dixter: The Nursery
greatdixter.co.uk

Knoll Gardens
knollgardens.co.uk

Leahurst Nurseries
treeferns.com

Naturescape
naturescape.co.uk

Pineview Plants
pineviewplants.co.uk

Special Plants Nursery
specialplants.net

Walled Garden Treberfydd
walledgardentreberfydd.com

Acknowledgments

Many thanks to Amy Gibson, Benjamin Kempton, Eelke Jan Bles, Elly Ward Morris, Lauren Fried, Marianne Morse, Matt Collins, Sacha Leong, and Susie Honeyman for letting us photograph their beautiful green spaces. And extra thanks to Louise Boyland and her lovely saluki (the real Linda) for sharing their courtyard.

First published in 2022 by Frances Lincoln
an imprint of The Quarto Group.
The Old Brewery, 6 Blundell Street,
London, N7 9BH, United Kingdom
www.Quarto.com

gardening · nature · inspiration

A Bloom book for Frances Lincoln
Bloom is an independent publisher for gardeners, plant admirers,
nature lovers and outdoor adventurers. Alongside books and stationery,
we publish a seasonal print magazine that brings together expert
gardening advice and creative explorations of the natural world.
Bloom celebrates all green spaces, from wilderness to windowsills,
and inspires everyone to bring more nature into their lives.
www.bloommag.co.uk | @bloom_the_magazine

Text © 2022 Susanna Grant
Photography © 2022 Aloha Bonser-Shaw
Illustrations © Botanical line art sketches by Madiwaso via Creative Market

Susanna Grant has asserted her moral right to be identified as the
Author of this Work in accordance with the Copyright Designs and Patents Act 1988.

Commissioning editor Zena Alkayat
Designer Sarah Pyke
Photographer Aloha Bonser-Shaw
Proofreader Joanna Chisholm
Indexer Michèle Clarke

A catalogue record for this book is available from the British Library.

ISBN 978-0-7112-6956-9

Printed in China

10 9 8 7 6 5 4 3 2

MIX
Paper from
responsible sources
FSC® C016973